mentor „sehr gut“

Englisch: sehr gut

6. Klasse

Gymnasium und Gesamtschule

Susan Bollinger
Angela Drude-Moss
Carola Jeschke

Mit Download für phase-6

Einfach ins Langzeitgedächtnis

In Zusammenarbeit mit Langenscheidt

mentor
Eine Klasse besser.

Die Autorinnen

Susan Bollinger, M.A., ist Diplomübersetzerin und unterrichtet ihre Muttersprache Englisch seit vielen Jahren an der Universität München; sie hat außerdem umfangreiche Unterrichtserfahrung an deutschen Schulen und als Nachhilfelehrerin und ist Autorin einiger Lernhilfen.

Angela Drude-Moss unterrichtet ihre Muttersprache Englisch seit vielen Jahren an der Universität München und hat außerdem mehrjährige Erfahrung in der Lehrerausbildung und im Nachhilfeunterricht.

Carola Jeschke ist Gymnasiallehrerin für Englisch und Deutsch und seit vielen Jahren mit der Erarbeitung von Unterrichtsmaterialien in beiden Fächern befasst.

Projektbetreuung: bookwise medienproduktion, München
Redaktion: Carolin Wolf, Regensburg
Layout: Cordula Schaaf, München
Umschlaggestaltung: Design im Kontor – Iris Steiner, München
Zeichnungen: Sabine Völkers, Berlin
Kapitel „Arbeit mit dem Wörterbuch“: in Zusammenarbeit mit der Langenscheidt-Redaktion
Lerneinheiten für den Download: Geraldine Tahmassebi

www.mentor.de
www.mentor.de/sehr-gut

Umwelthinweis: Gedruckt auf chlorfrei gebleichtem Papier.

Satz: Ute Konstanzer, München
Repro: Lana Repro, Lana
Gesamtherstellung: Druckerei A. Plenk, Berchtesgaden
Printed in Germany

ISBN 978-3-580-65226-5

1. 2. 3. 4. 5. 13 12 11 10 09

Inhalt

6 Adverbiale

7 Leseverstehen

8 Wortschatz und Situationen

Lösungen

★ Dieses Sternchen markiert Übungen und Regeln, die etwas anspruchsvoller sind oder nicht überall verlangt werden. Wenn du ganz sicher bist, dass du sie nicht brauchst, kannst du sie überspringen. Ansonsten gilt: Stell dich der Herausforderung!

1

Zeiten

Mrs Johnson's brother Alan Booth is married to an American and they live in Boston. The Johnsons are planning to visit their relatives in the summer holidays. The children are very excited as the family will hire a camper van and travel around to see some of the important places in American history, such as Washington and Philadelphia, and maybe even travel to the west, if there is time.

1.1 *Present Tense*/Präsens

Alles klar?! ***Revision: Simple Present/Present Progressive***
Wiederholung: Präsens/Die Verlaufsform des Präsens

Simple present/Präsens – eine Zeitform, mit der man über die Gegenwart spricht.

Das *simple present* wird verwendet:

- für regelmäßige und gewohnheitsmäßige Handlungen,
- bei Tatsachenbeschreibungen,
- bei Zustandsverben (z. B. *to know, to belong, to seem, to remember*).

*The Johnsons **go** on holiday every year.*

*The airport **is** near their home.*

*They **remember** all their holidays very well.*

*They **often go** in August.*

Signalwörter: *always, often, sometimes, never, every week, on Fridays*

- Bei Frage und Verneinung braucht man das Hilfsverb *to do*.
- Die Form der 3. Person Singular lautet: *does*.

***Do** they **go** on holiday at Easter?*

*No, they **don't**.*

Present progressive – eine Zeitform, mit der man über Handlungen spricht, die gerade stattfinden.

Das *present progressive* wird verwendet:

- für Handlungen, die gerade in diesem Moment stattfinden. **Signalwörter:** *at the moment, now, just, Look!*

*At the moment the Johnsons **are sitting** in their dining room and **are planning** their holiday in America.*

- Bei der Frage wandert das Hilfsverb vor das Subjekt.

*What **are** they **doing** in the dining room?*

- Bei der Verneinung wird das *not* an die Form des Hilfsverbs *to be* angehängt.

*They **aren't having** dinner.*

Übung 1 **Setze die Verben in die richtige Form der Gegenwart (*simple present* oder *present progressive*).**

1. The twins .... (to feed) the cat every morning. Today Mandy .... (to give) Maggie her food, because Mark .... (to look for) his school things.
2. It is Friday afternoon and Katie .... (to ride) Little Richard. She usually .... (to ride) him on Saturdays, but not this weekend as it is her mother's birthday.
3. Mrs Johnson often .... (to bake) a cake at the weekend. But today it is Katie and the twins who .... (to bake) two cakes for their mother's birthday.
4. Mandy and Mark .... (to have) a judo lesson every Friday. This week they .... (to practise) a new throw which they .... (to find) very difficult.
5. Mr Johnson .... (to like) to cycle to work every morning. But today it .... (to rain) hard so he .... (to go) by car.
6. Katie sometimes .... (to borrow) a book from the library on her way home from school. She is now in the library and .... (to look for) a book on horses.

Übung 2 **Beantworte die Fragen auf Englisch.**

1. How often do the Johnsons go on holiday?

   ....

2. When do they often go on holiday?

   ....

3. What are the Johnsons doing at the moment?

   ....

4. Where are they sitting?

   ....

5. Where is the dining-table?

   ....

6. Does Katie do her French homework at the dining-table?

   ....

7. Does Little Richard belong to Katie?

   ....

8. What do the Johnsons do every year?

   ....

Lösungen Seite 98

1.2 *Future Tense*/Futur

Alles klar?! ***Will-future*/Futur mit *will***

Während es im Deutschen nur eine Form – die Form mit *werden* – für das Futur gibt und auch das Präsens verwendet werden kann, um über Zukünftiges zu sprechen, gibt es im Englischen mehrere Möglichkeiten.

	Das *will-future* wird gebildet:
*It **will** be hot when they go.*	• mit *will* **und** • dem Verb im Infinitiv ohne *to* *Will* ist bei allen Personen gleich.
*It'**ll** be hot when they go.*	**Positiver Aussagesatz:** Hier kann die Kurzform *'ll* verwendet werden.
*It **will not** rain a lot.* *It **won't** rain a lot.*	**Negativer Aussagesatz:** Das *not* wird in Verbindung mit dem Hilfsverb gebraucht. Hier kann die Kurzform *won't* verwendet werden.
***Will** it **be** hot?*	Bei der **Frage** wandert das Hilfsverb vor das Subjekt.

	Das *will-future* wird verwendet:
*It **will** be very hot when they go.* *I think they **will** like their holiday very much.*	• für zukünftige Ereignisse, die man nicht beeinflussen kann, • für Vermutungen, Hoffnungen, Voraussagen.
	Signalwörter für diese Verwendung des *will-future* sind: *I think* .... *I suppose* .... *I hope* .... *I'm sure* .... *perhaps* .... *probably* ....
*They are hungry now. Dad **will** get some sandwiches.*	• für spontane Entscheidungen für die Zukunft.
	Weitere **Signalwörter** für *will-future*: *next (week, month, year ...)* .... *in (2050, three weeks1 ...)* .... *tomorrow* ....

Lösungen Seite 98

Übung 1 **Bilde Sätze mit den folgenden Ausdrücken und dem *will-future*.**

Die Familie Johnson plant einen Besuch bei ihren Verwandten in Boston.
Katie freut sich auf den Urlaub.

She believes that .../She hopes that .../She thinks that .../She is sure that ...

1. (her relatives be nice)
2. (her uncle meet them at the airport)
3. (the plane arrive on time)
4. (not be travel sick)
5. (the flight not take too long)
6. (her parents hire (= mieten) a camper van)
7. (the weather be fine in Boston)
8. (she see many interesting places)
9. (they have a lot of fun)
10. (her family enjoy the visit)

Beachte den Unterschied:
They will buy their tickets on the internet. = Sie werden ihre Tickets im Internet kaufen.
They want to buy their tickets on the internet. = Sie wollen ihre Tickets im Internet kaufen.

Lösungen Seite 98

Übung 2 **Setze das *will-future* ein.**

1. We have our tickets for the plane. We .... (to see) you at the airport.
2. We must leave now or we .... (to miss) the airport bus.
3. I think, we .... (to enjoy) our holiday in the USA.
4. Don't eat too much on the plane, Mark. You .... (to be) airsick.
5. I hope the weather .... (to be) fine in Boston.
6. Don't worry, we .... (to take) our umbrellas (= Regenschirme) just in case.

Übung 3 ★ **Formuliere Sätze mit dem *will-future*. Beachte die Wortstellung!**

1. It's rush hour. a lot of traffic/on the road to the airport/to be/there.

....

2. Next week there is a public holiday (= Feiertag) in the USA./come/to Washington/ the Booths/too.

....

3. Wait, the red light is on/to call/I/the stewardess

....

4. If the plane is late/not/to wait/Mr Booth/at the airport.

....

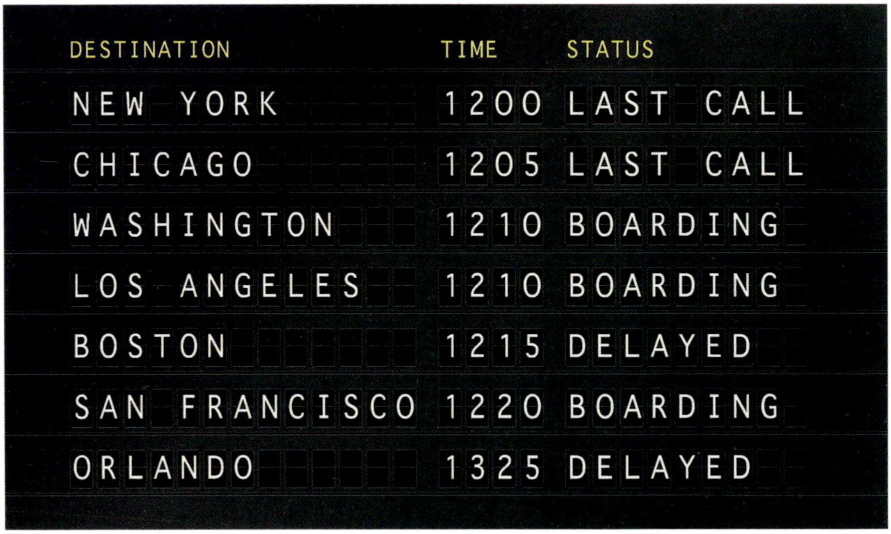

Lösungen Seite 99

Alles klar?! ***Going-to-Future*/Futur mit *going to***

	Das *going-to-future* wird gebildet: • mit einer Form von *to be* im Präsens (**Singular:** *I am, you are, he/she/it is* **Plural:** *we are, you are, they are*) und • *going to* **und** • dem Verb in der Grundform (Infinitiv)
*They **are going to hire** a camper van.* *They**'re going to hire** a camper van.*	**Positiver Aussagesatz:** Hier kann man die **Kurzform** verwenden: **Singular:** *I'm, you're, he's, she's, it's* **Plural:** *we're, you're, they're*
*They **aren't going to stay** in a hotel.*	**Negativer Aussagesatz:** Das *not* wird in Verbindung mit dem Hilfsverb gebraucht. Hier kann man die **Kurzform** verwenden: **Singular:** *I'm not, you aren't, he/she/it isn't* **Plural:** *we aren't, you aren't, they aren't*
***Are** they **going to visit** friends?*	Bei der **Frage** wandert das Hilfsverb vor das Subjekt.
	Das *going-to-future* wird verwendet für
*They **are going to hire** a camper van.*	• feste Vorhaben, Absichten, Pläne.
*Today, the children **are going to do** their homework in the evening.*	• Voraussagen über Ereignisse, die sich schon anbahnen und die mit großer Sicherheit eintreten werden.

Merke

In einem Satz mit dem Hauptverb *go* verwendet man anstelle des *going-to-future* häufig die Verlaufsform, da die Doppelung von *go* komisch klingen würde. Also: „*They are going by plane*“ anstatt „*They are going to go by plane*“.

Übung 4 **Setze die richtigen Formen des *going-to-future* ein.**

1. The Johnsons .... (to meet) their parents at the airport after school.
2. They .... (to fly) to Boston for their holiday.
3. Our parents promised: we .... (to hire) a camper van.
4. The holiday is all planned. We .... (to visit) Boston, Washington and Philadelphia.
5. Look at the clouds! It .... (to rain).
6. Katie has a brush in her hand. She .... (to brush) her horse.
7. Mrs Johnson called her brother on the phone. She .... (to visit) him in Boston.
8. The door of the plane is closing. The plane .... (to take off).

Lösungen Seite 99

Übung 5 ★ **Bilde Fragen in der passenden Form des Futur.**

1. .... (you/to spend) your holiday in Aviemore this year? – No, I'm not.
2. .... (Grandma Booth/to brush) my horse? – No, she won't. She's afraid of horses.
3. .... (the weather/to be) hot in Boston? – Yes, it will.
4. .... (to Boston/you/to fly) at the weekend? – Yes, I am.
5. .... (the flight/to take) more than six hours? – Yes, it will.
6. .... (your father/to hire) a camper van in Boston? – Yes, he is.
7. .... (you/to visit) other cities in America? – Yes, we are.
8. .... (you/to sleep) during the flight? – Yes, I will.
9. .... (you/to send) me a postcard from Boston? – Yes, I will.
10. .... (your uncle/to meet) your family at Boston Airport? – Yes, he is.

Lösungen Seite 99

1.3 *Past Tense*/Vergangenheit

Alles klar?! ***Revision: Simple past*/Wiederholung: Präteritum**

*Last year they **went** to Aviemore.*	Das ***simple past*** verwendet man für abgeschlossene Ereignisse in der Vergangenheit. **Signalwörter:** *yesterday, last week, two years ago*
***Did** they **go** to Brighton last year?* *No, they didn't.*	Bei **Frage** und **Verneinung** braucht man das Hilfsverb *to do* in der Vergangenheit *(did)*.

Übung 1 **Dieses Jahr verbringt die Familie Johnson den Urlaub in Amerika. Schreibe, was sie letztes Jahr gemacht haben.**

1. Katie .... (to get) riding lessons for her birthday.
2. The twins .... (to join) the school orchestra.
3. The family .... (to visit) the grandparents in London.
4. They .... (to go) on a trip to the Tower of London.
5. They .... (not/to go) on a boat trip on the Thames, because it was raining.
6. They .... (to see) the Changing of the Guard at Buckingham Palace.
7. Mrs Booth .... (to tell) the family about her son Alan in Boston.
8. Mr and Mrs Johnson .... (to decide) to spend their next holiday in America.

Alles klar?! **Bildung des *Present Perfect*/Perfekt**

Das *present perfect* entspricht zwar auf den ersten Blick dem deutschen Perfekt. Diese scheinbar ähnlichen Zeiten weichen jedoch in der Verwendung und in der Bedeutung stark voneinander ab. Während im Deutschen das Perfekt – vor allem in der gesprochenen Sprache – auch für lange zurückliegende Ereignisse verwendet werden kann, ist das englische *present perfect* eine Zeitform, die eine Verbindung von der **Vergangenheit zur Gegenwart** herstellt.

Lösungen Seite 99/100

Today the Johnsons ***have talked*** *about their plans for three hours.* *Katie* ***has asked*** *many questions.*	**Das *present perfect* wird gebildet:** • mit dem Hilfsverb *have* **Singular:** *I have, you have, he/she/it has* **Plural:** *we have, you have, they have* und • dem *past participle* (Partizip Perfekt)
The children ***have asked*** *a lot of questions.* *They* ***have copied*** *a lot of materials.* *They* ***have*** *also* ***phoned*** *some travel agents.* *They* ***have planned*** *what they are going to see in Boston.*	Bei der Bildung des *past participle* bei regelmäßigen Verben hängt man (wie bei der Bildung des *simple past*) an die Grundform des Verbs .... an: *talk*........, *ask*........ Beim Schreiben achtet man besonders auf: • Verben, die auf einen Konsonanten + *y* enden: Das *y* wird zu .... und du hängst .... an. • Verben, die mit einem stummen *-e* enden: Hier entfällt das .... • Verben mit kurzem, einfachem Vokal, auf den ein Konsonant folgt: Der Konsonant wird ....
Mum ***has written*** *down all the things they have to think about.*	Wie auch bei den Formen des *simple past* wird das *past participle* mancher Verben nicht regelmäßig gebildet. Diese Verben muss man so lange nachschlagen und lernen, bis man sie beherrscht. *write* → .... *do* → .... Das *past participle* ist immer die dritte Form in den Listen mit unregelmäßigen Verben, wie z. B. auch in der Liste auf Seite 124.
*They****'ve talked*** *about their plans.*	**Positiver Aussagesatz:** Hier kann man die **Kurzform** verwenden. **Singular:** *I've, you've, he's/she's/it's* **Plural:** *they've, you've, they've*
They ***haven't phoned*** *their uncle.*	**Negativer Aussagesatz:** Das *not* wird in Verbindung mit dem Hilfsverb gebraucht. Hier kann man die **Kurzform** verwenden: **Singular:** *I haven't, you haven't, he/she/it hasn't* **Plural:** *they haven't, you haven't, they haven't*
Have *they* ***checked*** *their passports?*	Bei der **Frage** wandert das Hilfsverb vor das Subjekt.

Lösungen Seite 100

Übung 2 **Setze das Verb in der Klammer in die richtige Form.**

1. Katie's horse is clean, she .... just .... (to brush) it.
2. "...................... you .... (to write) a letter to Uncle Alan?"
   "Yes, I .... already .... (to finish) it."
3. We .... (not/to be) to America yet.
4. Katie has French at school. She .... (to learn) it for two years now.
5. The Booths .... (to live) in Boston for three years.
6. Distances are so great in America. They .... (not/to visit) New York yet.
7. Mrs Johnson .... (to work) for the church for six years.
8. "............................ Katie .... (to go) to her riding lesson?"
   "Yes, she .... already .... (to leave)."
9. The twins .... (to feed) the cat.
10. "................ the Johnsons .... (to book) their flights?"
    "No, Mr Johnson .... (not/to phone) the travel agent yet."

Lösungen Seite 100

Alles klar?! **Verwendung des *Present Perfect*/Perfekt**

*They **have thought** about going to America for the last year.* *They **have thought** about going to America since Christmas.*	**Das *present perfect* wird verwendet:** • für Ereignisse oder Handlungen, die in der Vergangenheit angefangen haben und die bis an die Gegenwart heranreichen. **Signalwörter:** *since* + Zeitpunkt .... *for* + Zeitraum ....
*They **have just eaten** their sandwiches.*	• für Ereignisse, die gerade abgeschlossen worden sind. **Signalwort:** *just* ....
*Dad **has bought** some guidebooks.*	• für Ereignisse, die abgeschlossen sind, aber Auswirkungen auf die Gegenwart haben.
*Have **they already informed** their uncle?* *No, they **haven't informed** him **yet**.*	• für Ereignisse, die in der Vergangenheit stattfanden ohne Zeitangabe. **Signalwörter:** *not yet* .... *already* ....
*They**'ve managed** to talk about a lot of things **up to now**.*	**Weitere Signalwörter:** *so far* .... *up to now* .... *ever* .... *never* .... *today/this morning/week* (wenn dieser Zeitraum noch nicht vorbei ist) ....

Lerntipp

Wenn du das *past participle* eines unregelmäßigen Verbs vergessen hast, kannst auf Seite 124 nachschlagen. Dort findest du eine Liste mit Verben, die du laufend wiederholen solltest, bis du dir ganz sicher bist, wie die Formen lauten. Dann fallen dir die folgenden Übungen leichter.

Lösungen Seite 100

Übung 3 **Bilde Sätze aus den vorgegebenen Wörtern und Satzteilen. Was sagen dir die Signalwörter? Achte auf die Satzstellung.**

1. just: Mandy/to feed/the cat.

....

2. never: Anne/to see/a French film.

....

3. for: The Booths/to live/three years/in Boston.

....

4. already: We/to book/our flight to America.

....

5. not yet: The twins/to be/to Washington.

....

6. so far: Katie/to have/six riding lessons.

....

7. ever: you/to fly/in an aeroplane?

....

8. up to now: Maggie/to catch/six mice.

....

9. never: Uncle Alan/to visit/New York.

....

10. not yet: Mr Johnson/to drive/a camper van.

....

Lösungen Seite 100

Alles klar?! ***Past Progressive*/Die Verlaufsform der Vergangenheit**

*The Johnsons **were talking** about their trip to America, when the phone rang.*

Das *past progressive* wird gebildet:

- mit einer Form von *to be* in der Vergangenheit.

Singular: *I was, you were, he/she/it was*

Plural: *we were, you were, they were* **+**

- der *-ing*-Form

(= Grundform des Verbs + *-ing*, z. B. *read* + *-ing*).

Es wird also ähnlich gebildet wie das *present progressive*, nur dass die Form von *to be* in der Vergangenheit steht.

*I was **writing** a letter, when …*

*They were **planning** the trip when …*

*He was **lying** in his bed when …*

Beim Schreiben muss man beachten:

- Verben, die mit einem stummen *-e* enden: Hier entfällt das ....
- Verben mit kurzem, einfachem Vokal, auf den ein Konsonant folgt: Der Konsonant wird ....
- Verben auf *-ie*: Das .... wird zu einem ....

*They **were talking** about their trip from three to five.*

Das *past progressive* wird verwendet:

- wenn man Verlauf und Länge einer Handlung oder eines Vorgangs besonders betonen möchte.

*They **were talking** about their trip to America when the phone rang*

- für Handlungen, die während eines bestimmten Zeitraums in der Vergangenheit verlaufen. Sie bilden oft den „Hintergrund“ für einsetzende Ereignisse in der Vergangenheit, die im *simple past* stehen.

The telephone rang.

They were talking about their trip …

Übung 4 ***Simple past* oder *past progressive*? Setze das Verb in die richtige Form.**

On Sunday Katie .... (to sit) at her desk when her mother .... (to come) into the room. Katie .... (to write) a letter to her Uncle Alan in Boston about the trip to the USA the family .... (to plan). Katie and her mother .... (to talk) about their holiday when the phone .... (to ring). It was Uncle Alan. He .... (to ask) about the time of their flight and .... (to say) he .... (to hope) to meet them at the airport. Katie .... (to have) a test in French at school the next day. She .... (to learn) for the test after supper, while the twins .... (to play) monopoly. They .... (to be) also very excited about the holiday; while they .... (to play) monopoly they .... (to listen) to a programme about America on the radio.

Lösungen Seite 101

Übung 5 ★ **Setze die richtige Verbform ein.**

It .... (to be) Saturday afternoon and the Johnsons .... (to be) all at home because it .... (to rain). Katie .... (to read) a book while Mark .... (to do) his homework. He .... (to hope) that the rain .... (soon, to stop), because he and Ben .... (to watch) a football match in Canterbury. Mandy .... (to talk) to her mother about Uncle Alan. The Johnson children .... (not, to see) their uncle for a few years and they .... (never, to meet) his wife, Cindy. Mandy .... (to want) to know why her uncle .... (to go) to America and how he .... (to meet) Aunt Cindy. Mrs Johnson .... (to say) that he .... (to want) to work in America to gain experience (= Erfahrung sammeln) as a computer expert. While he .... (to look for) a job, he .... (to have) an interview (= Einstellungsgespräch) with a firm where Cindy .... (to work) as a secretary. Six months later they were married (= verheiratet). " .... (you, think) that Uncle Alan ....(ever, come) back to England to work?" Mandy asks. " .... (I, not, think) so," her mother replies, "he .... (to earn) much more money in America than he could ever earn in England."

Abschlusstest (30 Minuten)

STOPP! Zuerst die Lernkärtchen durcharbeiten!

Aufgabe 1 **Setze das Verb in der Klammer in die richtige Zeit.**

Tomorrow it .... (to be) cloudy in the morning and there .... (to be) heavy rain in the afternoon. In the evening our plane .... (to leave) for Boston. The flight .... (to take) nine hours and we .... (to arrive) early the next morning. Our relatives .... (to meet) us at the airport.

Punkte: ☐ von 6

Aufgabe 2 **Setze das *going-to-future* ein und kreuze die richtige Anwendung an.**

a) Festes Vorhaben, Verabredung, Plan, Entscheidung
b) Absehbare Voraussagen

1. Look, how grey the sky is! It .... (to snow). a) ❑ b) ❑
2. We .... (to visit) Boston this summer. a) ❑ b) ❑
3. Uncle Alan .... (to meet/not) us at the airport. His car has broken down. a) ❑ b) ❑
4. I'm tired of waiting. I .... (to leave) now. a) ❑ b) ❑

Punkte: ☐ von 8

Lösungen Seite 101

Aufgabe 3 **Setze das Verb in die richtige Zeit: *simple past* oder *present perfect*.**

Katie unterhält sich mit ihrer Mutter:

Mrs J: Where .... you .... (to be), Katie? It's already time for supper.

Katie: Sorry, I .... (to go) to Anne's house. We .... (to have) so much French homework that we .... (to forget) the time.

Mrs J: What .... you .... (to talk) about, your horses?

Katie: No, we .... (to discuss) our holidays. Do you know that Anne .... (to visit) America? .... you .... (to see) New York, Mum?

Mrs J: No, I .... (not/to visit) America, but your father and I .... (to go) to Scotland last year and we .... (to see) many other countries so far.

Katie: Oh, dear! And I .... (to explore only) London up to now.

Punkte: ☐ von 12

Aufgabe 4 **Stelle Fragen mithilfe der Verben in Klammern und der Signalwörter.**

Ben fragt Mark.

1. ever: .... (visit) America?
2. so far: .... (not have) breakfast ....?
3. never: .... (see) your American cousin?
4. already: .... (book) your flight?
5. just: .... (enter) the classroom?
6. not yet: .... (do) your homework?

Punkte: ☐ von 6

Lösungen Seite 101/102

Aufgabe 5 **Setze das Verb in der Klammer in die richtige Zeit.**

Mrs Booth tells her story:

My name .... (to be) Mary Booth, I .... (to live) in Wimbledon all my life. My husband and I .... (to buy) our house when we married and .... (to live) in it for thirty years. We .... (to marry) in 1960 and we .... (to have) two children. My daughter .... (to live) in Canterbury for ten years and my son Alan .... (to move) to America three years ago. Since then, he .... (to live) in Boston. While we .... (to have) supper last night, Alan .... (to phone) and .... (to tell) me that his sister and her family .... (to visit) him soon. He .... (to meet) them at the airport. During their visit they .... (to make) a trip to Washington and Philadelphia. It .... (to be) their first visit to America, but they .... (to be) to other countries in Europe and last year they .... (to go) to Scotland.

Punkte: ☐ von 18

Punkte: ☐ von 50

43–50: Bravo! Du weißt über die Zeiten schon gut Bescheid.
26–42: Teilweise bist du sicher, teilweise noch nicht. Bearbeite bitte noch einmal die Übungen, in denen du beim ersten Mal viele Fehler hattest.
0–25: Leider ist dir noch zu vieles unklar. Arbeite das Kapitel bitte noch einmal durch.

Lösungen Seite 102

2

Modale Hilfsverben

The Johnsons want to visit Philadelphia because it was at the centre of the American fight for independence from Great Britain in the 1770s. They hope to see Independence Hall where people from the thirteen North American colonies met to discuss how they could gain their freedom. On July 4th 1776 the Liberty Bell was rung to show the new American nation that they were free. Visitors to Philadelphia can also see the house of Betsy Ross, who sewed the first American flag with thirteen red and white stripes and thirteen stars.

2.1 *Modal Auxiliary Verbs*/Modale Hilfsverben

Alles klar?! **Was du über Hilfsverben wissen musst**

Einige Hilfsverben hast du schon kennengelernt:

- *to be,* das hilft, das *present progressive* zu bilden,
- *to have,* das hilft, das *present perfect* zu bilden,
- *will,* das hilft, das Futur zu bilden,
- *to do,* das hilft, Fragen oder Verneinungen zu bilden.

Neben diesen Hilfsverben gibt es die **modalen Hilfsverben**, wie z. B. *can, may, must.*

Sie drücken aus, ob Sprecher denken, dass das Subjekt eines Satzes etwas kann, darf, muss, also wie sie die Handlung, über die sie sprechen, persönlich einschätzen. Modale Hilfsverben haben folgende Eigenschaften:

- Sie können nur im ***simple present*** und teilweise im ***simple past*** verwendet werden. Deshalb werden sie auch manchmal unvollständige Hilfsverben genannt.
- In der 3. Person Singular wird kein ***-s*** angehängt.
- Sie können – außer bei Frageanhängseln und Kurzantworten – nie allein stehen, sondern sie brauchen immer ein Vollverb (ohne *to*).
- Bei **Fragen** und **Verneinungen** braucht man keine Umschreibung mit *to do*, denn die modalen Hilfsverben helfen selbst, Fragen und Verneinungen zu bilden.

Alles klar?! ***can/could*/Das Hilfsverb können**

*They **can go** to the science museum.* *Mr Johnson **could run** very fast when he was a boy.*	Die Bedeutung von *can/could* stimmt weitgehend mit dem deutschen „können“ überein. *Can* und *could* stehen immer mit einem Vollverb.
***Can** we **go** to the Betsy Ross House today?* *No, we **can't**.*	Bei der **Frage** wandert das Hilfsverb vor das Subjekt. Bei der **Verneinung** wird *not* an das Hilfsverb angehängt. Die verneinten Formen lauten: *can* → *cannot*, Kurzform: *can't* *could* → *could not*, Kurzform: *couldn't*

*Katie **can speak** French.* *You **can't leave** your coat here.* ***Can** we see an Imax film?* *This **can't** be true!* *We **can** see the film tomorrow.*	***Can* kann Folgendes ausdrücken:** • körperliche und geistige Fähigkeiten eines Menschen, • eine Erlaubnis bzw. ein Verbot, • eine Bitte, • eine Möglichkeit oder eine Unmöglichkeit, • Zukünftiges (mit einer Zeitangabe der Zukunft).
*Last year they **could see** the French coast from the pier in Brighton.* ***Could** we **go** to the Betsy Ross House today?*	***Could* kann Folgendes ausdrücken:** • Vergangenheit („konnte"), • Möglichkeit und Höflichkeit („könnte").
*They **have been able to see** a lot of sights.* ***Have** they **been able to go to** the science museum?*	*Can/could* als unvollständiges Hilfsverb kann nur im *simple present* und im *simple past* verwendet werden. Für alle anderen Zeiten brauchst du die Ersatzform ***to be able to***.

Merke

Da Hilfsverben immer mit einem Vollverb verwendet werden müssen, heißt „Ich kann Englisch": „I can speak English."

Übung 1 Beantworte die Fragen mit ***Yes, ... can/could*** oder ***No, ... can't/couldn't.***

Beispiel: Can Katie speak French? Yes, she can.

1. Could Mr Johnson run fast when he was a boy? ....
2. Can Maggie catch mice? ....
3. Can Mandy speak French? ....
4. Can Mandy and Mark play the recorder? ....
5. Could Katie speak French when she was two? ....
6. Can Mark keep his room tidy? ....

Lösungen Seite 103

Übung 2 ★ **Was bedeutet *can, can't (cannot), could, couldn't (could not)* in den folgenden Sätzen? Wähle jeweils eine der folgenden Bedeutungen:**
Fähigkeit; Fähigkeit verneint; Erlaubnis; Verbot; Bitte; Möglichkeit; Unmöglichkeit; Zukünftiges

1. Mandy: "Can I speak to Uncle Alan when he phones?" ....
2. Mrs Johnson: "Yes, you can, but don't speak for too long." ....
3. Mark to his father: "I can't believe it. Mandy spoke to Uncle Alan for over a quarter of an hour." ....
4. Mrs Johnson to Mandy: "You can't talk to Uncle Alan for so long next time. It is far too expensive." ....
5. Mandy: "But it was so interesting. Uncle Alan was telling me that when he first went to America, he couldn't always understand the way Americans speak English." ....
6 Mrs Johnson: "Your uncle is just too patient (= geduldig) with you. Next time you have so many questions, you could tell him that you will write him an e-mail." ....
7. Mandy: "I'm not going to write to him now. I can ask him everything I want to know when we reach Boston." ....
8. Mrs Johnson: "Well that could take some time! .... What a blessing (= Segen) that we can stay a few days with him and Aunt Cindy when we arrive next month." ....

Lösungen Seite 103

Übung 3 **Setze *can, can't (cannot), could, couldn't (could not)* ein.**

After staying with Alan and Cindy Booth for five days in Boston the Johnsons have now arrived in Philadelphia.

Mark and Mandy:	When .... we go to Independence Hall?
Mrs Johnson:	We .... go today or tomorrow.
Mark and Mandy:	We .... go tomorrow, because Uncle Alan will be in Philadelphia and he wants to go inline skating with us. .... you and Dad come, too?
Mrs Johnson:	You know, that your father .... skate.
Mandy:	But why .... he? I .... skate when I was eight.
Mark:	And I .... skate when I was seven.
Mrs Johnson:	Now, now you two. Your father has never learnt to skate. But you .... play the violin when you were five, ... you?

Alles klar?! ***may*/Das Hilfsverb dürfen**

*Visitors **may walk** on the grass.*	Mit *may* drückt man eine Erlaubnis (= „dürfen") aus. Es steht immer mit einem Vollverb.
***May** visitors **walk** on the grass?* *Yes, they **may**.*	Bei der Frage wandert das Hilfsverb vor das Subjekt.
***May** we **see** an Imax film?* *Yes, of course you may.*	Wenn du um Erlaubnis fragst, ist die Frage mit *may* höflicher als die Frage mit *can*.
***May** visitors **touch** the dinosaur? No, they may not.*	
*You **mustn't** touch the dinosaur.*	Wenn man etwas nicht darf, wird es zum Verbot. Die **strenge** Verneinung von *may* lautet deshalb ***mustn't***.
*They **have been allowed to do** a lot of experiments in the science museum.* ***Have** they **been allowed to do** a lot of experiments in the science museum?*	*May* ist ein unvollständiges Hilfsverb, und es kann nur im ***simple present*** verwendet werden. Für alle anderen Zeiten und ein nicht so strenges Verbot braucht man die **Ersatzform *to be allowed to***.

Lösungen Seite 103

Übung 4 **Beantworte die Fragen mit *Yes, ... may/must/have* oder *No, ... may not/haven't.***

Beispiel: May visitors sit on the grass? Yes, they may.

1. May Katie drive a car? ....
2. May Mrs Johnson drive a car? ....
3. May visitors touch the dinosaur? ....
4. Have Mark and Mandy been allowed to feed Maggie? ....
5. May cars drive at 100 kilometres per hour in towns? ....
6. May Mark draw pictures in his English lesson? ....

Übung 5 **Setze *may, may not, mustn't (must not), have been allowed* oder *have not been allowed* ein.**

Katie and her father are in the house of Betsy Ross.

For many years visitors to the Betsy Ross house .... to take photographs or use mobile phones. They .... walk everywhere, but they .... touch the exhibits (= Ausstellungsobjekte). Katie asks her father, "............................... we get nearer to the flag? I can't see it very well." "Yes, of course," her father says, "but not too close. You .... set the alarm off." Kate then asks her father, "............................... I take a photograph of the flag?" "No," he says, "you .... When we leave, we will buy a postcard of the flag."

Lösungen Seite 103

Alles klar?! ***must*/Das Hilfsverb müssen**

*They **must go** to the science museum.*	Die Bedeutung von *must* stimmt weitgehend (außer in der Verneinung) mit dem deutschen „müssen“ überein. Es steht immer mit einem Vollverb.
*You **needn't** go there. It's not interesting.*	Wenn man etwas nicht tun muss, braucht man es nicht zu tun. **Die Verneinung** von *must* lautet deshalb *needn't* (= „nicht brauchen“). ***Must* kann Folgendes ausdrücken:**
*You **must** leave now. The museum closes in five minutes.*	• eine Verpflichtung, ein Zwang, eine Notwendigkeit,
*You **must** be tired. It was a long day.*	• eine Wahrscheinlichkeit oder eine Gewissheit.
*They **had to leave** the museum at 6 pm.* ***Did** they **have to leave** the museum at 6 pm?* *They **didn't have to leave** the museum at six, because on Saturday the museum is open till 9 pm.*	*Must* ist ein unvollständiges Hilfsverb, es kann nur im ***simple present*** verwendet werden. Für alle anderen Zeiten braucht man die **Ersatzform *to have (got) to***. Da *have* in diesem Fall ein Vollverb ist, ist bei **Frage** und **Verneinung** die Umschreibung mit *to do* notwendig.

don't have to = nicht müssen – ***needn't*** = nicht brauchen – ***mustn't*** = nicht dürfen

Das ist eine Unterscheidung, die für uns Deutsche sehr schwierig ist. Deshalb sollest du dir hiervon Kärtchen oder Klebezettel mit Beispielsätzen machen, damit du dir die unterschiedlichen Bedeutungen gut einprägst:
You don't have to get up early tomorrow because it's Sunday.
You needn't get up before 9 am because we won't leave before 10 am.
You mustn't stay up late tonight because of your English test tomorrow.

Übung 6 ★ Setze *must, needn't, have to* ein.

1. Which sights .... the Johnsons see when they are in Philadelphia?
2. Visitors .... leave the museum now. It closes in 10 minutes.
3. Mr Johnson .... buy a postcard of the flag. His wife bought one yesterday.
4. Why .... the Johnsons .... leave the museum at 6 pm?

   Because on Saturday it was open until 9 pm.
5. You haven't eaten anything all day. You .... be hungry.
6. .... you .... pay to see the Liberty Bell? No, I didn't. It is free.

Übung 7 Übersetze die modalen Hilfsverben ins Englische.

Since 11th September 2001 Independence Hall und the Liberty Bell are in a security zone (= Sicherheitszone). Visitors .... (müssen) go through a security check. They .... (müssen) put their coats and bags in the cloakroom (= Garderobe) and they .... (müssen) pass through a special door, which checks for metal objects. The Johnsons .... (mussten) wait half an hour at the security check, but they .... (mussten nicht) show their tickets again. The attendant said, "You .... (brauchen nicht) show me your tickets. I checked them when you first came into the museum."

Lösungen Seite 104

STOPP!
Zuerst die Lernkärtchen durcharbeiten!

Abschlusstest (30 Minuten)

Aufgabe 1 **Übersetze die Sätze ins Englische.**

1. Wir können morgen ins Museum gehen.

   ....

2. Besucher dürfen nicht fotografieren.

   ....

3. Mark konnte schwimmen, als er sieben war.

   ....

4. Können wir ein Eis haben?

   ....

5. Die Johnsons könnten die Liberty Bell um 10 Uhr sehen.

   ....

6. (Am Abend) Wir haben heute viele Sehenswürdigkeiten sehen können.

   ....

7. Sie konnten letztes Jahr nicht nach Amerika fahren.

   ....

Punkte: ☐ von 14

Aufgabe 2 **Setze *must, needn't, had to, did, have to* ein.**

1. We .... visit Independence Hall when we are in Philadelphia.
2. You .... get to the museum before 9 o'clock because it doesn't open until 9.15.
3. When the Johnsons reached the museum they .... put their coats and bags in the cloakroom.
4. .... Mr Johnson .... switch off his mobile phone? – Yes, he did.
5. At the end of the day Mark asked, "............................. we walk back to the camper van? I am so tired."
6. "No, we .... walk. We can catch a bus."

Punkte: ☐ von 6

Lösungen Seite 104

Aufgabe 3 **Setze *can, can't (cannot), could, to be able to, may, must, mustn't (must not), to have to, needn't* ein.**

1. .... we have an ice cream? Yes, but you .... eat it before we go to look at the Liberty Bell. Visitors .... eat anything in the Liberty Bell Center.
2. Mandy asks an attendant, "................... we draw a picture of the Liberty Bell?" "Yes, you ...., but you .... stop other visitors from seeing the bell. You .... sit at the side of the room."
3. The Johnsons are sitting at the side of the room and Mark and Mandy are drawing a picture of the bell. Suddenly Mrs Johnson's mobile phone rings and she answers it. It is her brother. He wants to know, when the children .... go inline skating. An attendant sees Mrs Johnson telephoning and tells her that she .... use her mobile phone in the Center. "But you .... end your call," he says, "you .... go outside to telephone."
4. Now Mrs Johnson is outside. She says to her brother, "They .... go with you later today, but tomorrow is better." "Then we will go tomorrow," he replies.
5. That evening Mrs Johnson tells her husband that she was very cross, because she .... go outside the Center to telephone. "But it has been a lovely day and we .... see a lot of sights," she says.

Punkte: ☐ von 14

Punkte: ☐ von 34

30–34: Bravo! Du weißt über die Hilfsverben schon gut Bescheid.
20–29: Teilweise bist du sicher, teilweise noch nicht. Bearbeite bitte noch einmal die Übungen, in denen du beim ersten Mal viele Fehler hattest.
0–19: Leider ist dir noch zu vieles unklar. Arbeite das Kapitel bitte noch einmal durch.

Lösungen Seite 104

3

Pronomen

Alan Booth takes his visitors on a trip to New York, where he has also never been. The children are particularly excited about seeing Times Square and Broadway, they also hope they might get tickets for a musical, their favourite would be “Cats”. While in New York, they will also try to visit Harlem as Katie has been learning all about the problems of the Afro-Americans and the Civil Rights movement in her history lessons at school.

3.1 *Indefinite Pronouns*/Indefinitpronomen

Alles klar?! ***some* and *any***

They wanted ***some*** *information about* ***some*** *Broadway shows.* *They didn't see* ***any*** *baseball matches.*	Mit *some* und *any* macht man eine unbestimmte Mengenangabe. Wenn *some* mit zählbaren Nomen, wie z. B. *shows*, verwendet wird, bedeutet es „einige“, „ein paar“, wenn es mit unzählbaren Nomen, wie z. B. *information*, verwendet wird, bedeutet es „etwas“.
They had ***some*** *drinks in the cafeteria.* *Could I have* ***some*** *more coke?*	***Some*** **wird verwendet:** • in bejahten Sätzen, • in höflichen Fragen und in Fragen, auf die man eine positive Antwort erwartet.
They didn't have ***any*** *sandwiches.* *Did they have* ***any*** *lunch?*	***Any*** **wird verwendet:** • in verneinten Sätzen, • in neutralen Fragen.
Are there ***any*** *sandwiches left? – No, there aren't* ***any***.	*Some* und *any* können auch ohne Substantiv verwendet werden.

Übung 1 **Setze *some* oder *any* ein.**

1. Katie has bought .... postcards.
2. Mrs Booth is feeding .... cats.
3. The twins have not got .... shoes on.
4. There isn't .... milk in the fridge.
5. Mark and Mandy have bought .... cakes for tea.
6. Mr Johnson can't read the map, he is not wearing .... glasses.

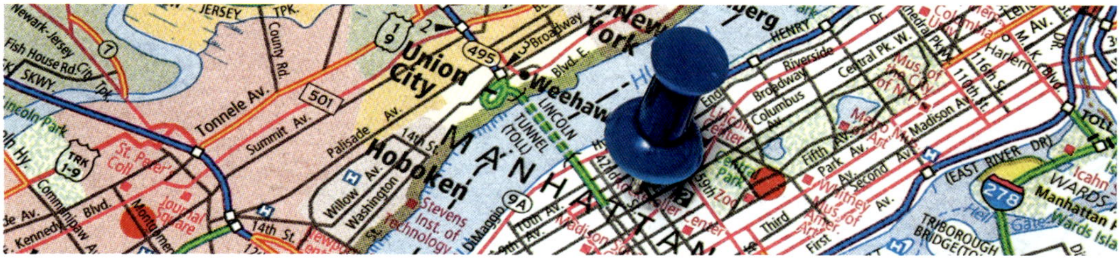

Lösungen Seite 105

Alles klar?! ***some* and *any* in Zusammensetzungen**

Mit *some* und *any* können auch Zusammensetzungen gebildet werden, für die die gleichen Verwendungsregeln gelten.

*They wanted to talk to **somebody/someone**, but there wasn't **anybody/anyone**.*	für Personen: ***somebody/someone*** ***anybody/anyone*** deutsch: (irgend)jemand
*They wanted to go **somewhere** exciting.* *The first night they were so tired that they didn't want to go **anywhere**.*	für Orte: ***somewhere*** ***anywhere*** deutsch: (irgend)wo, (irgend)wohin
*The lady at the information desk showed them **something** on the map. They couldn't see **anything** interesting at that theatre.*	für Dinge, Gegenstände: ***something*** ***anything*** deutsch: (irgend)etwas

Übung 2 **Setze eine sinnvolle Zusammensetzung von *some* oder *any* ein.**

Katie: I am very hungry, Mum. Can I have .... to eat, please?

Mark: I can't see Mandy ...., but I know she is in the van ...., because I can hear her.

Mark: Is there .... there? I heard .... cough (= husten).

Mr J.: I can't find my sunglasses ...., may I have yours?

Mrs J.: No, you may not, I'm not going to lend (= leihen) you .... again, because you never give things back.

Lösungen Seite 105

Übung 3 ★ **Setze eine sinnvolle Zusammensetzung mit *some* oder *any* ein.**

Mark: Mandy, listen! I think .... is outside the camper van.

Mandy: Don't be silly, Mark. I can't hear ....

Mark: Are you sure? I definitely heard ....

Mandy: No, you didn't. There isn't .... outside.

Mark: Has Uncle Alan said .... about a visit to New York yet?

Mandy: I think so. He said .... to Dad at supper last night.

Mark: Oh dear, I can't find the guidebook (= Reiseführer) for New York ....

Mandy: Well, it can't disappear. It must be .... in the van.

Mark: Does Uncle Alan know .... in New York?

Mandy: I don't think so. He hasn't said ....

Mark: Isn't it fun! We have never done .... so exciting before.

Mandy: We have never been .... as exciting as America before!

Lösungen Seite 105

Alles klar?! **Die Pronomen *each/every***

*They went to Broadway **each/every** day.*	*Every* und *each* bedeuten beide *jeder/jede/...*, wobei *each* eher die Getrenntheit von Dingen, Personen betont („jeder Einzelne") und *every* eher die Gruppenzugehörigkeit betont („jeder/alle"). Mit *every* können Zusammensetzungen gebildet werden.
***Everybody** was really happy.*	für Personen: ***everybody/everyone*** deutsch: jeder, alle
*They wanted to go **everywhere.***	für Orte: ***everywhere*** deutsch: überall, überallhin
*And they wanted to see **everything**.*	für Dinge, Gegenstände: ***everything*** deutsch: alles

Übung 4 **Setze das passende Wort in die Lücke: *each/every/everybody/everything/anywhere.***

While the Johnsons were in New York they stayed in a small hotel. They got up early .... day and had breakfast in a café only a few metres from their hotel. .... in the family was enjoying their trip to New York. They wanted to see .... of interest, go ...., but they had little time and they could only do a few things .... day. They were really tired .... evening when they went to bed, but after only a few hours of sleep they were ready to go ....

Lösungen Seite 105

Alles klar?! **Zusammensetzungen mit *no***

Auch mit *no* können Zusammensetzungen gebildet werden.

*There was **nobody/no one** they could ask.*	für Personen: ***nobody/no one*** (= *not anyone*) deutsch: keiner, niemand
*Mandy was **nowhere** to be seen.*	für Orte: ***nowhere*** (= *not anywhere*) deutsch: nirgends, nirgendwo
*There was such a storm that they could see **nothing**.*	für Dinge, Gegenstände: ***nothing*** (= *not anything*) deutsch: nichts

Übung 5 **Setze das passende Wort in die Lücke: *nobody/no one/nowhere/nothing***

Die Johnsons wollen nach New York fahren, sie haben aber Probleme.

1. Mr Johnson wants to start the camper van, but the petrol tank is empty. There is .... in the tank.
2. They are strangers in Boston and do not know where to get petrol. It is very early in the morning and there is .... around to ask.
3. The streets are deserted (= leer), there is .... around.
4. Katie looks for the map (= Karte), but it is .... to be seen.
5. It was still early when they finally set off and it was so foggy (= neblig) that Mr Johnson could see ....

Lösungen Seite 105

Übung 6 ★ **Benutze Zusammensetzungen von *no* oder *any*, um die Fragen ablehnend und in ganzen Sätzen zu beantworten.**

Beispiel: What did you buy in New York? I didn't buy anything.

1. What is wrong with the camper van? ....
2. Did you see anybody at the garage? ....
3. What did you do? ....
4. Where did you go? ....
5. Who did you ask for help? ....
6. What did the garage man tell you? ....
7. What can I do to help? ....
8. Where was the map in the van? ....
9. What did you pay the garage man? ....
10. Where did you take the van? ....

Lösungen Seite 106

3.2 *Indefinite Numeral Adjectives*/Indefinite Zahladjektive

Alles klar?! ***much/many/a lot of***

Mit *much/many/a lot of* macht man Mengenangaben.

*They didn't get **much** sleep. Everything was so expensive in New York; they spent too much money.*	*Much* bedeutet „viel" und wird verwendet: • mit unzählbaren Substantiven, • v. a. in negativen Sätzen und Fragen, • in Verbindung mit *too, very, so* auch in bejahten Aussagesätzen.
*Did the Johnsons visit **many** interesting sights?*	*Many* bedeutet „viele" und wird verwendet: • mit zählbaren Substantiven im Plural, • v. a. in negativen Sätzen und Fragen, • in Verbindung mit *too, very, so* auch in bejahten Aussagesätzen.
*They went to **a lot of** shows.*	*A lot of* (verkürzte Form: *lots of*) bedeutet „viel/viele" und wird verwendet: • mit unzählbaren Substantiven und zählbaren Substantiven im Plural, • v. a. in bejahten Aussagesätzen und Fragen.

Übung 1 **Setze ein passendes indefinites Zahladjektiv ein.**

The trip to New York

1. The camper van was not very big. There was not .... room in it for the family.
2. They were pleased to be in New York as there were .... things to do there.
3. They saw Times Square and Broadway and visited .... museums.
4. They did not see Harlem as they did not have .... time.
5. How .... musicals did they see?
6. Katie did not buy any souvenirs. She spent too .... money on postcards.

Lösungen Seite 106

Alles klar?! ***little/few/a few***

Mit *little/few* macht man Mengenangaben.

*There was too **little** time to see everything.*	*(A) Little* bedeutet „(ein) wenig" und wird verwendet: • mit unzählbaren Substantiven. Es ist somit sozusagen das „Gegenstück" zu *much*.
*There were only **few** tickets left.*	*Few* bedeutet „wenige" und wird verwendet: • mit zählbaren Substantiven im Plural. Es ist somit sozusagen das „Gegenstück" zu *many*.
*The weather was good for **a few** days.*	*A few* bedeutet „einige" und wird verwendet • mit zählbaren Substantiven im Plural.

Übung 2 **Übersetze die unterstrichenen Wörter ins Englische.**

1. Die Familie Johnson verbringt ein paar Tage in New York. ....
2. Sie hat keine Pläne für den Abend. ....
3. Sie haben viele Sehenswürdigkeiten gesehen. ....
4. Katie nimmt nur ein wenig Milch in Tee. ....
5. Es gab nur noch wenige Plätze im Theater. ....
6. Auf dem Times Square waren viele Leute. ....
7. Sie hatten zu wenig Zeit, um nach Harlem zu fahren. ....
8. Die Zwillinge hatten nicht viel Schlaf auf der Reise. ....

Lösungen Seite 106

STOPP!
Zuerst die Lernkärtchen durcharbeiten!

Abschlusstest (35 Minuten)

Aufgabe 1 **Wie sagt man dazu auf Englisch?**

etwas Benzin ....

kein Benzin ....

viel Benzin ....

wenig Benzin ....

wenige Verwandte ....

ein paar Verwandte ....

keine Verwandte ....

viele Verwandte ....

viel Zeit ....

wenig Zeit ....

etwas Zeit ....

keine Zeit ....

Punkte: ☐ von 12

Aufgabe 2 **Setze *some, any* oder eine ihrer Zusammensetzungen ein.**

1. I haven't got .... coffee, but you can have .... tea.
2. Mrs Johnson can't find her purse ...., but it must be .... in the camper van.
3. Mark is so lazy, he never does .... work in the house.
4. Have you got .... money with you in New York?
   Not here, but I've got .... at home in Boston.
5. Can .... in Washington speak French?
6. Anne can lend Katie .... books about horses.
7. Katie hasn't got .... books about horses yet.
8. There's .... wrong with our camper van. Can Uncle Alan do .... about it?

Punkte: ☐ von 12

Lösungen Seite 106

Aufgabe 3 **Formuliere die Sätze anders.**

Beispiel:
Katie is happy about nothing. Katie isn't happy about anything.

1. She wants to see no friends. ....
2. She talks to nobody. ....
3. She goes nowhere. ....
4. She does nothing. ....
5. She wants to see nobody. ....

Punkte: ☐ von 5

Aufgabe 4 **Setze die korrekten englischen Wörter ein.**

The twins must help to get things ready for the trip to New York because Uncle Alan has got only a .... (wenig) time today. There are .... (viele) things on the list. They must buy .... (ein paar) apples and .... (einige) oranges for the journey and .... (etwas) sugar and .... (etwas) coffee. They must also buy two bottles of milk, because there isn't .... (keine) milk in the fridge in the camper van. Is there perhaps .... (irgendetwas) they have forgotten? Yes, they must also buy .... (einige) maps in the bookshop. And where else must they go? They have thought of .... (alles); they needn't go .... (nirgends) else. If the family gets thirsty on the journey, they can stop and buy .... (ein paar) bottles of coke or water as there will be .... (nichts) to drink in the fridge except milk.

Punkte: ☐ von 13

Lösungen Seite 107

Aufgabe 5 **Setze *many, much, a little* oder *a few* ein.**

Am Ende der Reise nach New York.

1. There is only .... milk left.
2. In the bag you will find .... apples left.
3. How .... kilometres are on the clock (= Tacho)?
4. I haven't got .... petrol left in the tank.

Punkte: ☐ von 4

Aufgabe 6 **Übersetze die Sätze ins Englische.**

1. Wir brauchen etwas Milch.

....

2. Ich sah niemanden auf der Straße.

....

3. Könnte ich etwas zu trinken bekommen?

....

4. Habt ihr etwas in Harlem gesehen?

....

5. Deine Sonnenbrille ist irgendwo im Bus.

....

6. Hast du viel Kuchen gegessen?

....

Punkte: ☐ von 12

Punkte: ☐ von 58

50–58: Bravo! Du weißt über die Pronomen schon gut Bescheid.
30–49: Teilweise bist du sicher, teilweise noch nicht. Bearbeite bitte noch einmal die Übungen, in denen du beim ersten Mal viele Fehler hattest.
0–29: Leider ist dir noch zu vieles unklar. Arbeite das Kapitel bitte noch einmal durch.

Lösungen Seite 107

4 Adjektive und Adverbien

The Johnsons have now flown to San Francisco to see the sights in and around the city. Mr Johnson wants to find out all he can about the earthquake in 1906. Mrs Johnson hopes to see the famous Californian Redwoods, which are enormous trees that can live for over 2,000 years. Mandy and Mark are looking forward to taking a boat trip to Alcatraz Island, which was a prison for dangerous criminals until 1963. All the Johnsons are eager to see the Golden Gate Bridge, which is still one of the longest bridges in the world, and, of course, they want to travel on the famous cable cars.

4.1 *Adjectives*/Adjektive

Alles klar?! ***Position of Adjectives*/Stellung der Adjektive**

*Golden Gate Bridge is really **big**. The cable car is very **old**.*	**Adjektive** beschreiben Personen, Lebewesen, Dinge und Ereignisse genauer.
*It is a really **big** bridge.*	Wenn Adjektive Nomen näher beschreiben, stehen sie direkt vor dem Nomen. Man spricht in diesem Fall von **attributivem Gebrauch**.
*Golden Gate Bridge **is** really **big**. It **looks great** in fog.*	Bei bestimmten Verben kann das Adjektiv auch hinter dem Prädikat stehen. Hierzu gehören: • Verben, die einen Zustand beschreiben *to be* .... *to remain* .... *to become* .... *to seem* .... *to get* .... *to stay* .... *to grow* .... • Verben der Sinneswahrnehmung *to look* .... *to sound* .... *to feel* .... *to taste* .... *to smell* .... Die Adjektive beziehen sich in diesem Fall auf das Subjekt des Satzes. Man spricht von **prädikativem Gebrauch**. *The bridge is big.* *The bridge looks great.*

Lösungen Seite 108

Übung 1 **Setze ein passendes Adjektiv und den richtigen Artikel zu einem Substantiv.**

Beispiel: a blue flower

blue tall
happy green sleepy
red big fast
old

flower train
cable car tree bridge
leaf cat rose boy

Übung 2 **Bilde Sätze.**

1. looks/nice/Katie's new dress
2. Mandy/happy/is feeling
3. has grown/Maggie/fat
4. old/is getting/Mr Booth
5. untidy/Mark's room/is
6. tastes/nice/this ice cream

Lösungen Seite 108

Alles klar?! ***Comparison of Adjectives*/Steigerung der Adjektive**

*Sydney Harbour Bridge is **long**, Brooklyn Bridge is **longer**, Golden Gate Bridge is **the longest** of the three.*	Die meisten Adjektive lassen sich steigern. Damit kann man Menschen, Dinge, Ereignisse vergleichen. **Positiv (Grundstufe):** *long* **Komparativ (1. Steigerungsstufe):** *long**er*** **Superlativ (2. Steigerungsstufe):** *long**est***
*It is **nicer** to see Golden Gate Bridge in good weather.* *Golden Gate Bridge is **bigger** than Brooklyn Bridge.* *It is **easier** to travel across the bridge by car.*	Steigerung mit ***-er, -est***: • bei einsilbigen Adjektiven • bei zweisilbigen Adjektiven auf *-y, -le, -er, -ow.* Bei der Schreibung ist zu beachten: • Adjektive, die mit einem stummen *-e* enden: Hier entfällt das Steigerungs-*e*. • Adjektive mit kurzem, einfachem Vokal, auf den ein Konsonant folgt: Der Konsonant wird *verdoppelt*. • Adjektive, die auf *-y* enden: Das *y* wird zu einem *i*.
*Katie thought that San Francisco was the **most interesting** city she had ever seen, even **more interesting** than New York.*	Steigerung mit ***more*** und ***most***: zweisilbige Adjektive, die nicht auf *-y, -le, -er, -ow* enden, sowie andere mehrsilbigen Adjektive
*San Francisco is **as expensive as** New York.* *Are the skyscrapers **higher** in New York **than** in San Francisco?*	Wenn man mehrere Dinge miteinander vergleicht, dann verwendet man bei der • Grundstufe: ***(not) as*** + Adjective + ***as***. • 1. Steigerungsstufe: Adjective (in 1. Steigerungsstufe) + ***than***. **Achtung Verwechslungsgefahr:** *than* = als, *then* = dann.

Lerntipp

Bei der Steigerung von Adjektiven gibt es wieder unregelmäßige Formen, die du lernen musst:

good – better – best | *little – smaller – smallest*

bad – worse – worst | *little – less – least*

Übung 3 **Vervollständige die Tabelle mit den richtigen Steigerungsformen der Adjektive.**

Grundstufe	Komparativ	Superlativ
high		
		nicest
	easier	
big		
	more expensive	
interesting		
		most exciting
beautiful		
	simpler	
sad		

Übung 4 **Setze die vorgegebenen Adjektive in die richtige Form (Grundstufe, Komparativ oder Superlativ).**

1. It is a hot day today. It is .... than yesterday.
2. It is often foggy in San Francisco. It is the .... place in California.
3. New York is very cold in winter. It is .... than San Francisco.
4. New York is an exciting city, but it is not as .... as San Francisco.
5. There is a fast train to New York, but it is .... to go by plane.
6. Mandy has just watched a sad film. It was the .... film she has ever seen.
7. The Eiffel Tower is tall, but the Empire State Building is ....
8. Katie is a good horse rider, but Anne is .... than her.
9. French lessons are interesting. They are .... than maths lessons.
10. Ben is a bad football player. He is the .... player in the team.

Lösungen Seite 108

4.2 *Adverbs*/Adverbien

Alles klar?! ***Adverbs of Manner*/Adverbien der Art und Weise**

*They walked **slowly** across Golden Gate Bridge.*

Adverbien der Art und Weise beschreiben eine Handlung oder ein Geschehen genauer. Sie beziehen sich somit auf Verben.

Adverbien werden gebildet, indem man ***-ly*** an ein **Adjektiv** hängt.

slow → *slowly*

Bei der Schreibung ist zu beachten:

*Katie wrote **happily** to her friend about her trip.*

*There was **simply** so much to see.*

***Realistically** they couldn't expect to see all the sights they wanted to see.*

- Bei Adjektiven, die auf *-y* enden, wird die Adverbendung zu *-ily*.
- Bei Adjektiven, die auf *-le* enden, wird die Adverbendung zu *-ly*.
- Bei Adjektiven, die auf *-ic* enden, wird die Adverbendung zu *-cally*.

*They are **fast** walkers.*

*They walked **fast** to catch the train.*

Adverbien, die die gleiche Form wie Adjektive haben:

early	....	*long*	....
fast	....	*low*	....
high	....		

*They could **hardly** see anything, because of the fog.*

*In summer tourist guides have to work really **hard**.*

Adjektive mit doppelten Adverbien:

Adjektiv	**1. Adverb**	**2. Adverb**
hard (= hart, schwer)	*hard* (= hart, schwer)	*hardly* (= kaum)
late (= spät)	*late* (= spät)	*lately* (= in letzter Zeit)
near (= nahe)	*near* (= nah)	*nearly* (= fast, beinahe)

Beachte den Unterschied!

Das Adverb von *good* heißt *well*; *well* kann aber auch ein Adjektiv sein, dann bedeutet es „gesund": *He can speak English very well./He isn't feeling well today.*

Lösungen Seite 109

Übung 1 **Bilde Adverbien aus den folgenden Adjektiven und setze sie ein.**

quick | slow | real | careful | clear | eager | easy | lucky | terrible

1. Mandy and Mark are .... looking forward to the trip to Alcatraz Island.
2. They run .... to the boat.
3. The boat crosses San Francisco Bay ...., because there are many other boats nearby.
4. The captain steers (= lenken) the boat .... round the rocks.
5. He speaks .... so that the passengers can .... hear what he says about the murderers in Alcatraz prison.
6. ...., Mandy and Mark do not feel frightened by the captain's stories.
7. When the boat returns to San Francisco, they are .... hungry.
8. "Did you enjoy the trip?" Mrs Johnson asks the twins. "Oh yes, it was .... exciting."

Übung 2 ★ **Adjektiv oder Adverb? Unterstreiche die Adjektive und Adverbien und bestimme, ob es sich um ein Adjektiv oder ein Adverb handelt.**

1. Anne does not let her horse jump over high fences. ....
2. Mark threw the ball up high. ....
3. Mark does not like to get up early. ....
4. Katie likes to take the early bus to school. ....
5. Yesterday she did not take long to do her homework. ....
6. It was a long journey for the Johnsons from New York to San Francisco. ....
7. It's better to take the fast train. ....
8. Mark and Mandy had to run fast to catch the boat. ....

Lösungen Seite 109

Übung 3 **Setze die richtige Form der Adverbien ein.**

late/lately hard/hardly near/nearly

1. Ben lives .... Mark.
2. Katie could .... see the first American flag in the Betsy Ross house.
3. Mr Johnson has read a lot of books on earthquakes ....
4. Katie and Anne have .... finished their homework.
5. Mandy was angry with Mark, because they were .... for school.
6. Mark does not work very ....

Alles klar?! ***Comparison of Adverbs*/Steigerung der Adverbien**

*They even walked **more slowly** across Golden Gate Bridge, when they came back.*

Die **Steigerung** der meisten Adverbien wird mit *more* und *most* gebildet:

slowly – more slowly – most slowly

Auch bei der Steigerung von Adverbien gibt es unregelmäßige Formen, die man lernen muss:

well – better – best:

.... – .... – ....

badly – worse – worst:

.... – .... – ....

Übung 4 **Übersetze die Adverbien ins Englische.**

1. When the bus reached Golden Gate Bridge, it drove .... (langsamer).
2. Cable cars do not travel .... (schneller) than buses.
3. Cars can travel .... (am schnellsten) on motorways.
4. Ben plays football .... (am schlechtesten) when he is the goalkeeper.
5. He plays .... (besser) when he is a defender (= Verteidiger).
6. Mark plays .... (am besten) when he can score a goal.

Lösungen Seite 109/110

STOPP!
Zuerst die Lernkärtchen durcharbeiten!

Abschlusstest (25 Minuten)

Aufgabe 1 **Unterstreiche die Adjektive und bestimme, ob sie attributiv (A) oder prädikativ (P) gebraucht werden.**

1. Mandy gets angry when Mark is late. **A P**
2. The Redwoods are the tallest living things on earth. **A P**
3. Golden Gate Bridge is the longest bridge the Johnsons have ever seen. **A P**
4. Mandy asks her father, "Is there a longer bridge anywhere in the world?" **A P**
5. There are not many old buildings in San Francisco, because the terrible earthquake in 1906 destroyed (= zerstören) most of them. **A P**
6. Have you heard the latest news about the forest fires? Yes, it sounds awful. **A P**

Punkte: ☐ von 9

Aufgabe 2 **Setze die folgenden Adjektive bzw. Adverbien an die passende Stelle.**

tallest | beautiful | calm | oldest | longer | old | fast | long | happy | tall | spectacular | early

Mrs Johnson has been to see the Californian Redwoods. These trees grow very .... and very .... The .... can live for over 2,000 years and the .... can reach 115 metres high. Mrs Johnson got up .... to catch the bus to the Redwood State Park. The bus drove .... along the coastal highway, but it was still a .... journey. When they arrived Mrs Johnson walked round the park and felt very .... to see the .... trees. On the journey back the bus had to take a .... route, because of forest fires. Mrs Johnson remained quite .... Later that evening she said to her husband, "The trees looked really .... What a pity that you didn't come, too."

Punkte: ☐ von 12

Lösungen Seite 110

Aufgabe 3 **Setze die Komparativ- oder Superlativform der Adjektive ein.**

Mr Johnson is reading about the earthquake in 1906. It was one of the .... (destructive) natural disasters ever, but the fire that followed was even .... (bad). It was .... (frightening) for the people of San Francisco than the earthquake, because they had .... (little) water than they needed to extinguish it (= löschen). The .... (terrible) thing was that nearly everyone lost their home. Today an earthquake is .... (likely = wahrscheinlich) to occur (= passieren) in the San Francisco area than in the rest of America.

Punkte: ☐ von 6

Aufgabe 4 **Bilde Sätze.**

Beispiel: Mandy is a slow walker. She walks slowly.

1. Katie is a careful rider. She ....
2. Mr Johnson is a fast cyclist. He ....
3. Anne is a good rider. She ....
4. Mrs Johnson is a hard worker. She ....
5. Ben is a bad football player. He ....
6. Mandy is a beautiful singer. She ....

Punkte: ☐ von 6

Punkte: ☐ von 33

27–33: Bravo! Du weißt über die Adjektive und Adverbien schon gut Bescheid.
18–26: Teilweise bist du sicher, teilweise noch nicht. Bearbeite bitte noch einmal die Übungen, in denen du beim ersten Mal viele Fehler hattest.
0–17: Leider ist dir noch zu vieles unklar. Arbeite das Kapitel bitte noch einmal durch.

Lösungen Seite 110

5

Satzformen

The Johnsons hire another camper van, because they want to see more of California. The children have heard a lot of things about the Californian lifestyle, the beach parties and the Spanish influence on the architecture. They want to see Los Angeles and Katie hopes she will catch sight of a famous film star in Hollywood. Mr and Mrs Johnson are more interested in nature and plan to visit the Grand Canyon and Yosemite National Park.

5.1 *Conditional Clauses (If-Clauses)*/Konditionalsätze (Typ I)

Alles klar?! ***If-Clauses***

If *you come to California, you* ***will*** *have a great holiday.*

Konditionalsätze bestehen aus zwei Teilen:

If *you come to California,*	*you* ***will*** *have a great holiday.*
einem **Nebensatz**, der eine Bedingung angibt	einem **Hauptsatz**, mit dem die Folge der Bedingung ausgedrückt wird
Einleitende Konjunktion ***IF*** (= wenn; falls)	(*then* = dann)

Hauptsatz und Nebensatz können vertauscht werden.
Wenn der Hauptsatz an zweiter Stelle steht, wird meist ein Komma gesetzt.
Konditionalsätze (Typ I) drücken **tatsächliche** oder **mögliche Ereignisse** und **Situationen** in der **Zukunft** aus.

Bei der Bildung ist auf die **Zeiten** in **Haupt-** und **Nebensatz** zu achten:

Nebensatz	**Hauptsatz**
If you come to California,	you will have a great holiday.
…………………………………………	…………………………………………

Tipp

If und *when* können beide mit „wenn" übersetzt werden. Zur Unterscheidung ist es aber hilfreich, eine weitere Übersetzungsmöglichkeit zu testen:

If you come to California …	*If* bezeichnet eine Bedingung. Eine andere Übersetzungsmöglichkeit ist „falls".
When you come to California …	*When* bezeichnet den Zeitpunkt, wann etwas geschieht. Eine andere Übersetzungsmöglichkeit ist „sobald".

Lösungen Seite 111

Übung 1 **Setze die richtige Verbform ein.**

1. If the Johnsons .... (to want) to see California, they .... (to need) a camper van.
2. If they .... (to visit) Santa Barbara, they .... (to see) many Spanish-type houses.
3. If Katie .... (to go) to Hollywood, she .... (to take) a bus.
4. Uncle Alan .... (to catch) the train into Boston at 8 am, if he .... (to leave) now.
5. If Mark .... (to eat) too many biscuits in the van, he .... (to feel) sick.
6. The Johnsons .... (to spend) the night in Carmel, if they .... (to find) a camping site.
7. They .... (to remember) Clint Eastwood, if they .... (to stop) in Carmel.
8. They .... (to see) many seals (= Robben), if they .... (to take) the Pacific coastal road.

Übung 2 **Bilde vollständige Konditionalsätze aus den beiden Spalten.**

if-Satz	Hauptsatz
Katie (to stay) longer	she (to be) angry
The twins (to go) to bed at 10 pm	they (to spend) two days in L.A.
The Johnsons (to have) enough time	she (to miss) the Hollywood bus
Mr Johnson (to tell) Mrs Johnson the cost of the van	they (to be) tired the next morning

If Katie stays longer, ...

If ....

If ....

If ....

Lösungen Seite 111

Übung 3 ★ **Übersetze die Wörter in Klammern ins Englische.**

1. Die Johnsons werden einen Campingplatz suchen, wenn (sobald) es dunkel wird. ....
2. Onkel Alan wird enttäuscht sein, wenn (falls) er keine Postkarte bekommt. ....
3. Wenn (falls) die Zeit reicht, werden sie Santa Barbara besuchen. ....
4. Wenn (sobald) sie in L.A. sind, werden sie Sunset Boulevard aufsuchen. ....
5. Katie wird Anne viel zu erzählen haben, wenn (falls) sie einen Rodeo sieht. ....
6. Die Familie wird nach L.A. fahren, wenn (sobald) sie den Grand Canyon besucht haben. ....

 Lösungen Seite 111

Alles klar?! ***Negative Conditional Clauses (If-Clauses)*/Verneinte Konditionalsätze (Typ I)**

*You **won't** (= will not) **miss** the dolphin show if you get there early enough.*	**Verneinter Hauptsatz:** Das ***not*** wird an das Hilfsverb angehängt.
*You will miss the dolphin show if you **don't get** there early enough.*	**Verneinter Nebensatz:** Wenn kein Hilfsverb vorhanden ist, verwendet man, wie sonst auch, die Umschreibung mit ***to do***.
*You **won't get** tickets for the dolphin show if you **don't get** there early enough.*	Auch beide Teile können verneint sein.

Übung 4 **Bilde vollständige Sätze aus den Teilsätzen in den Wolken.**

You (not, to enjoy) the trip
You (not, to have) time for the Grand Canyon
You (not, to see) the sunset over the Pacific
You (to miss) the plane

if

you (not, to stay) awake
you (to stay) too long in Yosemite
you (not, to get) to the airport on time
you (to get) car sick

....

....

....

....

....

Lösungen Seite 111

5.2 *Relative Clauses*/Relativsätze

Alles klar?! **Relativsätze**

*This is one of the pictures **which** Katie took of the Grand Canyon.*	**Relativsätze** werden in der Regel durch ein **Relativpronomen** eingeleitet. Das Relativpronomen verweist auf ein **Nomen** oder **Pronomen**, das im vorausgegangenen Satz verwendet wurde. Der Relativsatz macht so weitere Angaben zu den Nomen oder Pronomen. *All the tourists **who** visit the Grand Canyon are very impressed.* *Katie put all her stuff into the basket **which** she bought from the Indian.*
*Katie put all her stuff into the basket **that** she bought from an Indian.* *The Indian, **whose** shop was right at the entrance of the National Park, wore colourful clothes.*	Relativpronomen im Englischen: ***who(m)*** verweist auf Personen ***which*** verweist auf Dinge ***that*** verweist auf Personen und Dinge ***whose*** verweist auf Personen und zeigt Besitzverhältnisse an *(wessen?)*

Übung 1 **Unterstreiche den Relativsatz und schreibe das Relativpronomen auf.**

1. A camper van is a vehicle which is large. ....
2. Mrs Booth, who lives in London, is Katie's grandmother. ....
3. California is a state which has a lot of sunshine. ....
4. Mark, who is a twin, looks just like his sister Mandy. ....
5. This is the camping site that is cheapest. ....
6. People who live in California are called Californians. ....
7. Uncle Alan is the man whose home is in Boston. ....
8. Katie is the girl whose friend has a horse. ....

Lösungen Seite 111

Übung 2 **Vervollständige die Sätze mit Satzteilen, die du aus den Texten in den Wolken bildest. Setze das richtige Relativpronomen ein.**

to write books

to be cheap

to need a lot of petrol

to love horses

to be famous for its film stars

to have a sister in Canterbury

1. Alan Booth is a person ....
2. A camper van is a vehicle ....
3. Katie is a girl ....
4. Travelling by camper van is a way of having a holiday ....
....
5. Hollywood is a place ....
6. An author is someone ....

Lösungen Seite 112

5.3 *Question Tags*/ „Frageanhängsel“

Alles klar?! ***Question Tags***

The Grand Canyon is great, ***isn't it****?*	Möchte man sich nach einem Aussagesatz der Zustimmung des Gesprächspartners versichern, verwendet man im Englischen sogenannte ***question tags***. Im Deutschen sagt man dann einfach: „…, nicht wahr?“
	Ist das Verb im Hauptsatz bejaht, ist das *question tag* verneint; ist das Verb im Hauptsatz verneint, ist das *question tag* bejaht. *She* ***took*** *many photos,* ***didn't she****?* .... *She* ***didn't take*** *many photos,* ***did she****?* ....
They ***won't*** *return before the end of the holidays,* ***will they****?*	Enthält das Prädikat im Hauptsatz ein Hilfsverb, so wird es im *question tag* wiederholt.
You really ***like*** *the Grand Canyon,* ***don't you****?*	Enthält das Prädikat im Hauptsatz kein Hilfsverb, so wird im *question tag* die entsprechende Form von *to do* benötigt.

Übung 1 **Ergänze mit dem richtigen *question tag*.**

1. Katie took this photo of Yosemite National Park, ... ?
2. Mr and Mrs Johnson will spend two days in the Grand Canyon, ... ?
3. They won't visit Las Vegas, ... ?
4. The twins didn't visit Hollywood, ... ?
5. You really will fill the tank with petrol, ... ?
6. Santa Barbara is not very far from L.A., ... ?
7. San Francisco is a really beautiful city, ... ?
8. You won't forget to send Uncle Alan a card, ... ?
9. The twins have got many friends, ... ?
10. Katie doesn't drive the camper van, ... ?

Lösungen Seite 112

STOPP! Zuerst die Lernkärtchen durcharbeiten!

Abschlusstest (25 Minuten)

Aufgabe 1 **Setze die fehlenden Verben in der richtigen Zeit ein.**

1. If Katie .... (to walk) faster, she .... (to get/not) wet.
2. If we.................................. (to leave) now, we .... (to be) in L.A. at midday.
3. If we .... (to go) to the Grand Canyon, we .... (to see) bears.
4. Katie .... (to be) a good horse rider if she .... (to practise) more.
5. If you .... (to wait) for me, Mark, I .... (to help) you do the washing up.
6. Mandy .... (to post) a card to her friend at home if she .... (to find) a post-box.

Punkte: ☐ von 12

Aufgabe 2 **Setze die passenden Relativpronomen ein.**

1. Mrs Booth is the lady .... son lives in Boston.
2. Avis is the company .... provided the camper van.
3. Katie, is this your jacket .... is lying on the floor?
4. Is Mr Johnson the man .... hired the camper van?
5. Alan Booth is the man .... family is visiting from England.
6. Look at the man .... is climbing the mountain in Yosemite.

Punkte: ☐ von 6

Lösungen Seite 112/113

Aufgabe 3 **Setze *if* oder *when* und die richtige Zeitform ein.**

1. Uncle Alan .... (to be) at the airport .... our plane from L.A. .... (to land).
2. Katie .... (to take) a photograph .... she .... (to see) a bear in the park.
3. Mark and Mandy .... (to want) to see the dolphins .... they .... (to visit) San Diego.
4. Mr and Mrs Johnson .... (to go) walking in Yosemite .... they ... . (to have) time.

Punkte: [ ] von 12

Aufgabe 4 **Übersetze ins Englische.**

1. Du wirst mir helfen, nicht wahr?

   ....

2. Wenn du den Kühlschrank sauber machst, koche ich das Mittagessen.

   ....

3. Katie ist das Mädchen, das gerne reitet.

   ....

4. Mark und Mandy sind die Kinder, deren Onkel in Boston lebt.

   ....

5. Die Johnsons hatten einen schönen Urlaub in Amerika, nicht wahr?

   ....

6. Katie interessiert sich für Kinofilme, nicht wahr?

   ....

Punkte: [ ] von 12

Punkte: [ ] von 42

37–42: Bravo! Du weißt über die Themen in diesem Kapitel schon gut Bescheid.
22–36: Teilweise bist du sicher, teilweise noch nicht. Bearbeite bitte noch einmal die Übungen, in denen du beim ersten Mal viele Fehler hattest.
0–21: Leider ist dir noch zu vieles unklar. Arbeite das Kapitel bitte noch einmal durch.

Lösungen Seite 113

6

Adverbiale

After visiting the very busy Grand Canyon National Park the Johnsons want to relax at an Indian reservation for one or two days. Mr Johnson hopes to do some fishing and Mrs Johnson and Katie want to go horse riding in the beautiful lands of the Hualapai Indians (pronounced Wa-la-pie). Mark and Mandy are keen to find out about the Indian way of life, both past and present, but most of all they want to stay at this reservation so that they can have another look at the Grand Canyon, this time from the glass Skywalk that opened in 2007.

6.1 *Adverbials*/Adverbiale

Alles klar?! **Bildung der Adverbialen**

Mit dem *Adverbial* kann man die näheren Umstände eines Geschehens, wie den Ort, die Zeit, den Grund, genauer angeben. Das Adverbial ist – wie Subjekt und Objekt – ein eigenständiges Satzglied, das allerdings nicht zwingend ist und im Satz zusätzliche Informationen gibt.

Adverbiale können aus verschiedenen Wörtern und Wortgruppen gebildet werden:

First *they went* ***left, then*** *they went* ***right****, finally they saw the sign to the reservation.*	• aus Adverbien, sie sind unveränderbar.
Mr Johnson drove very ***slowly****.*	• aus Adverbien, abgeleitet von Adjektiven (vgl. hierzu auch Seite 52–54).
They arrived there ***in the evening.*** *Visitors to the Skywalk walk* ***on a thick glass floor****.* *Mr Johnson went fishing* ***the next day****.*	• aus einer Präposition und einem Nomen, das durch Beifügungen erweitert sein kann. • Bei manchen Adverbialen fehlt die Präposition.
They reached the reservation ***before it closed.***	• aus Adverbialsätzen, d. h. Nebensätzen, die durch eine Konjunktion eingeleitet werden.

Übung 1 **Übersetze die Adverbien in Klammern ins Englische.**

The Johnsons are .... (jetzt) driving to the Indian reservation. Mark and Mandy are tired and Mandy asks, "When will we get .... (dort)?" Her mother replies, "We'll be there .... (bald)." But the road .... (nie) seems to end. "Have we .... (jemals) been on a road that is as bumpy (= holprig) as this?" Mark asks. "No, ... (nie)," Katie says. "That's not .... (ganz) true," their father answers. "We .... (oft) drive along bumpy roads in England, but this camper van is .... (sehr) old and so we can feel every bump."

.... (Endlich) Mrs Johnson sees the sign to the reservation; they have .... (nur) 10 kilometres to go. After they have turned .... (links) and .... (dann) .... (rechts), they reach the Hualapai reservation. Everyone is very pleased that the journey is over.

Lösungen Seite 114

Übung 2 **Bilde Adverbien aus den folgenden Adjektiven (in Klammern).**

Mrs Johnson has written a card to her brother Alan in Boston. This is what she wrote:

We were wrong; the journey was not .... (real) over. We had to walk almost .... (vertical) for one kilometre down a very steep (= steil) path to the village. As we had all our bags with us, we could only walk very .... (slow). We .... (final) reached the village in the evening and we were by now all very hungry. We .... (immediate = unverzüglich) started to look for somewhere to eat, but there wasn't a restaurant anywhere. .... (Lucky) an Indian family saw us and asked, "Can we help you?" I .... (quick) told them how hungry we were. "............................ (sad) we don't have any restaurants here," they said. "But if you come with us, we will .... (glad = froh) give you something to eat." We followed the kind Indians to their house. There we .... (hungry) ate a delicious meal and .... (happy) accepted their invitation to stay the night after we learnt that we needed a tent to sleep in, which we had .... (unfortunate = unglücklich) forgotten.

Lösungen Seite 114

Alles klar?! **Adverbialen haben verschiedene Bedeutungen**

*They went **to the reservation**.*	Angabe zum Ort: **lokales** Adverbial	**Wo? Wohin? Woher? …**
*They arrived there **in the evening**.*	Angabe zur Zeit: **temporales** Adverbial	**Wann? Wie oft? Wie lange? Seit wann?**
*Mr Johnson drove very **slowly**.*	Angabe der Art und Weise: **modales** Adverbial	**Wie? Auf welche Weise?**
*Mr Johnson drove very slowly, **because of the bad roads**.*	Angabe des Grundes: **kausales** Adverbial	**Warum?**

Übung 3 **Vervollständige die Sätze mit Adverbialen aus einer Präposition und einem Nomen mithilfe der folgenden Informationen.**

The Hualapai Tribe
Hualapai (pronounced Wa-la-pie) means "People of the Tall Pines". The Hualapai live on a reservation which stretches over 4,000 square kilometres (= Quadratkilometer). The Hualapai people believe that the world began near here at "Spirit Mountain". The number of people in the Hualapai Tribe is 1,532. The men mostly work in the tourism industry and in cattle ranching (= Viehzucht). The women also work in the tourism industry and in the tribe's arts and crafts (= Kunstgewerbe) shops making and selling traditional Indian clothes and ornaments.

1. What does the name of the Hualapai mean? It means "People ....".
2. Where does the tribe live? They live ....
3. Where do the Hualapai believe that the world began? They believe that it began
   ....
4. How large is the Hualapai tribe? The number of people .... is 1,532.
5. Where do the men work? They work ....
   ....
6. Where do the women work? They work ....
   ....

Lösungen Seite 114

6.2 *Adverbial Clauses*/Adverbialsätze

Alles klar?! ***Adverbial Clauses***

They reached the reservation, ***before it closed.***	**Temporalsatz** (Zeit)	Einleitende Konjunktion: *when, after, before, as soon as*
Mark and Mandy liked the reservation very much, ***because they are interested in Indians.***	**Kausalsatz** (Grund)	Einleitende Konjunktion: *because*
If I go to America, *I will also go to an Indian Reservation.*	**Konditionalsatz** (Bedingung) (vgl. hierzu auch Seite 58–61)	Einleitende Konjunktion: *if*
They went to a reservation ***where they saw a lot of interesting things.***	**Lokalsatz** (Ort)	Der Lokalsatz stellt eine Besonderheit dar, weil er nicht durch eine Konjunktion, sondern durch ein Relativpronomen eingeleitet wird. Er gehört also zu den Relativsätzen (vgl. hierzu auch Seite 62).

Übung 1 **Unterstreiche die Adverbialsätze.**

Mark and Mandy want to see the Grand Canyon from the glass Skywalk because they hope that it will be very exciting to stand on the thick glass floor, which juts out (= hinausragen) 20 metres, and look down at the Canyon. Some visitors are quite afraid and desperately hold on to the glass walls. The twins are sure that they will walk fearlessly across the Skywalk if their parents will take them to see it. Mr Johnson does not really want to go to the Skywalk because he thinks that it will be very expensive.

Lösungen Seite 115

Übung 2 **Fülle die Lücken in den Fragesätzen.**

1. Why .... Mr Johnson ....?
   Because the roads were very bad.
2. When .... the Johnsons ....?
   They reached the village in the evening.
3. Where .... the Johnsons ....?
   They had a delicious meal in the house of a kind Indian family.
4. When .... Mrs Johnson ....?
   She reserved the horses early in the morning.
5. Why .... the twins .... ?
   Because they think it will be exciting to stand on the glass floor and look down at the Canyon.
6. Why .... Mr Johnson ....?
   Because he thinks that it will be very expensive.

Übung 3 ★ **Vervollständige die folgenden Sätze mit der passenden Konjunktion.**

until | before | after | when | because | as soon as

1. The Johnson children got very tired .... it was a long journey to the reservation.
2. The Johnsons were all very hungry .... they finally reached the village.
3. .... they arrived, they started looking for somewhere to eat.
4. The Johnsons thought, that they could hire a tent .... the Indian family told them that visitors have to bring one with them.
5. Early in the morning .... the rest of the family woke up, Mrs Johnson reserved two horses for Katie and herself to go riding the whole day.
6. .... it stopped raining, they went riding.

Lösungen Seite 115

Übung 4 **Bilde sinnvolle Sätze.**

Mrs Johnson reserved two horses	before he went fishing.
Mandy is going to write another postcard to her uncle	if she can find one that is not too expensive.
The twins are sure that they will be able to learn a lot about Indian culture	where the Canyon is not too steep.
Mr Johnson made sure that the twins had something to do	because he doesn't want to pay for the family to visit the Skywalk.
Mark wants to find out how Indians used to hunt	as soon as she woke up.
Katie wants to buy a bracelet (= Armband) from the arts and crafts shop	when she returns home.
The twins will be very disappointed	before she flies back to England.
Mrs Johnson is cross with her husband	if their friends have time to show them round the village.
Katie is looking forward to riding Little Richard again	while he is staying at the reservation.
Mrs Johnson and Katie want to ride the horses	if they cannot go to the Skywalk.

Lösungen Seite 115

Abschlusstest (30 Minuten)

STOPP! Zuerst die Lernkärtchen durcharbeiten!

Aufgabe 1 **Übersetze die Zeitadverbialen ins Englische.**

1. When they arrived at the Indian village .... (am Abend), they were very tired.
2. .... (Am nächsten Morgen) Katie and the twins did not wake up very early.
3. Mrs Johnson reserved two horses for Katie and herself to go riding .... (den ganzen Tag).
4. Mr Johnson promised the twins that they could visit the Skywalk .... (am nächsten Tag), if it wasn't too expensive.
5. He said to them, "I want to go fishing .... (am Nachmittag). What are you going to do?"
6. "Our Indian friends, Don and Tobey, are going to show us the village, and we will see how Indians lived .... (in der Vergangenheit) and how they live .... (heute)."

Punkte: ☐ von 7

Aufgabe 2 **Setze die Adverbialen an die richtige Stelle.**

kindly | excitedly | really | happily | traditionally | brightly | beautifully | next week | with great enthusiasm | on Friday

Don and Tobey have .... given the twins a photo album to look at, in which they can see pictures of an Indian powwow. ...., this is a meeting of Indian tribes where the chieftains (= Häuptlinge) talk about important things in the biggest wigwam and the tribes celebrate Indian culture by singing and dancing. Mark and Mandy are looking .... at all the photos, because Indian life .... interests them. The twins can see that some Indians are dancing .... and that others are talking and singing. The .... coloured costumes, which are .... decorated with feathers and beads (= Perlen), fascinate them most of all. "We are having a powwow ....," Don tells the twins. "Can you stay until then?" "Oh no", Mark says sadly, "we are flying to Boston ...." "Well, perhaps we could take you to meet our chieftain instead," Tobey says. The twins are thrilled and accept ....

Punkte: ☐ von 10

Aufgabe 3 **Beantworte die Fragen.**

1. Where do the twins see pictures of an Indian powwow?
   They ....
2. Why are the twins looking at the photos excitedly?
   Because ....
3. Where do the chieftains talk about important things?
   They ....
4. How do the Indians celebrate their culture?
   They ....
5. How do some of the Indians dance?
   They ....
6. When are the Johnsons flying to Boston?
   They ....

Punkte: ☐ von 12

Lösungen Seite 116

Aufgabe 4 **Bilde Adverbien aus sechs der Adjektive in Mandys Erzählung und setze sie an die richtige Stelle.**

That evening the twins told their parents about their exciting day. "The Hualapai chieftain, who is Don and Tobey's grandfather, is very old and wise. He was very kind to us and told us when and why the Indians came to the reservation," Mandy said, "but he also seemed to be very sad about this. He showed us some very old arrows (= Pfeile) and spears (= Speere), and then some beautiful costumes that he and his family will wear at the powwow next week. He was unhappy to hear that we won't be able to go, and has given us a farewell present (= Abschiedsgeschenk). We can visit the Skywalk tomorrow for free. Aren't we lucky?"

1. The Indian costumes were .... decorated.
2. ...., the twins are going to miss (= verpassen) the powwow, but they are now .... able to visit the Skywalk.
3. The Hualapai chieftain .... invited the twins to visit the Skywalk for free.
4. ...., the twins forgot to take a photo of the chieftain.
5. Mr and Mrs Johnson .... got up early to pack their bags.

Punkte: ☐ von 6

Punkte: ☐ von 35

30–35: Bravo! Du weißt über Adverbiale schon gut Bescheid.
19–29: Teilweise bist du sicher, teilweise noch nicht. Bearbeite bitte noch einmal die Übungen, in denen du beim ersten Mal viele Fehler hattest.
0–18: Leider ist dir noch zu vieles unklar. Arbeite das Kapitel bitte noch einmal durch.

 Lösungen Seite 116

7

Leseverstehen

The Johnsons have now returned to Canterbury after their stay in the USA. For Mark and Mandy, however, the trip does not seem to be completely over. They cannot forget their meeting with the chieftain of the Hualapai Indians and the sad expression on his face when he told them about the time that the tribe had to move to the reservation. Since their return the twins have been keen to find out all they can about the history of the Indians in America. This chapter will give you some ideas about how to get the most out of this kind of reading text.

*7.1 Reading and Understanding/*Lesen und Verstehen

Übung 1 **Texte erfassen**

Der folgende Text gibt Informationen über die Geschichte der Indianer; es handelt sich um einen *factual text*, einen Sachtext. Du erfasst den Text am besten, wenn du die Schlüsselbegriffe unterstreichst.

This is what Mark and Mandy have found out about the history of the American Indians or Native Americans as they are also called. Read through the text quickly without trying to understand every word and then underline the keywords. You will find the first ones already marked.

The story of the American Indians

<u>The Indians</u> had lived <u>in America for thousands of years</u> when the <u>Europeans</u> started to <u>arrive</u> in the <u>17th century</u>. At that time there were about 12 million Indians living there in more than one thousand different tribes.

At first the Indians welcomed the settlers enthusiastically. They found their white faces, their unusual clothes and their fine ships fascinating as well as the many things the settlers brought with them to start a new life.

In the early days the settlers found it difficult to grow food in the 'New World' and it was often the Indians who helped them to survive. But as time went on, conflicts began to develop between the Native Americans and the newcomers. The main reason for the wars that followed was the fight for land. The settlers wanted to own the land and use it themselves. They did not want to allow the Indians to graze their animals and grow crops on it anymore. The Indians, for their part, wanted to live in harmony with nature and they did not like the way the settlers made money out of the land and all it produced, like the buffalo, the trees, and the coal and iron deposits.

Many of the Native Americans died from the European illnesses which the settlers brought with them. Those who survived were not able to defend their lands against the large numbers of settlers, who fought in a well-organised army. The newcomers steadily drove the Indians from one place to another and took more and more of their lands for farming. With the loss of their lands many tribes also lost their large buffalo herds, which used to roam the prairie and provide the Indians with food, clothing and other things they needed. The settlers did not look after the buffalo, which were now on their lands, but killed them to sell their hides (= Fell). By the end of the 19th century the buffalo were almost extinct (= ausgestorben).

In the end, the United States government gave land to each of the Indian tribes: the Indian Reservations. But the land was often very poor and the Indians could not grow much food on it. This was a situation that made all Indians very sad. Today, there are one or more Indian reservations in every state. The Hualapai, in the end, is lucky to own the rocky land around a part of the Grand Canyon. People from all over the world visit this beautiful place and happily pay to walk on the new Skywalk, which, in a way, is the Hualapai's 'new buffalo'.

Lösungen Seite 117

Lerntipp
Es ist nicht schlimm, wenn du nicht alle Wörter verstehst. Bevor du in ein Wörterbuch schaust, versuche die Bedeutung selbst herauszufinden. Du kannst die Bedeutung vielleicht ableiten:
- aus dem Textzusammenhang,
- wenn du ein Wort aus der gleichen Wortfamilie kennst,
- aus einem ähnlichen deutschen Wort.

Übung 2 ★ **Fasse den Inhalt des Textes in wenigen Sätzen zusammen.**

....

....

....

....

....

....

....

Übung 3 **Versuche, die Bedeutung der folgenden Wörter zu erfassen, ohne im Wörterbuch nachzuschlagen.**

settler (Z. 4):	....	to survive (Z. 8):	....
conflict (Z. 8):	....	to develop (Z. 9):	....
fight (Z. 10):	....	to own (Z. 10):	....
to graze (Z. 11):	....	crops (Z. 11):	....
buffalo (Z. 13):	....	newcomer (Z. 9):	....
deposit (Z. 14):	....	iron (Z. 14):	....
illness (Z. 15):	....	to defend (Z. 16):	....
herd (Z. 19):	....	to roam (Z. 20):	....

Lösungen Seite 117

Übung 4 **Wortfamilien: Bilde die Adjektive zu den folgenden Substantiven.**

Beispiel: beauty beautiful

1. enthusiasm ....
2. fascination ....
3. difficulty ....
4. illness ....
5. sadness ....
6. luck ....
7. rock ....
8. happiness ....

Übung 5 **Finde den gegensätzlichen Begriff zu den folgenden Adjektiven.**

1. white ....
2. difficult ....
3. good ....
4. large ....
5. poor ....
6. lucky ....
7. ugly ....

Übung 6 **Lies den Text jetzt genauer durch und beantworte die folgenden Fragen.**

1. What fascinated the Indians about the settlers?

....

2. Why did conflicts develop between the Indians and the settlers?

....

3. What didn't the Indians like about the settlers?

....

4. Why did many of the Indians die?

....

5. Why were the settlers able to take away the Indians' land from them?

....

6. What did the American government do to solve the problem?

....

7. Why is the Skywalk called the Hualapai's 'new buffalo'?

....

Lösungen Seite 118

STOPP!
Zuerst die Lernkärtchen durcharbeiten!

Abschlusstest (25 Minuten)

Aufgabe 1 **Wortfamilien: Bilde das Verb zu den folgenden Substantiven.**

Beispiel: organisation to organise

1. settler	....	6. fight	....
2. loss	....	7. owner	....
3. life	....	8. production	....
4. growth	....	9. death	....
5. development	....	10. visitor	....

Punkte: ☐ von 10

Aufgabe 2 **Lies den Text noch einmal durch und beantworte die folgenden Fragen.**

1. How long had the Indians lived in America when the Europeans arrived?

   ....

2. How many Indians lived in each tribe on average (= im Durchschnitt)?

   ....

3. How did the Indians help the settlers to survive at first?

   ....

4. What didn't the settlers want the Indians to do anymore?

   ....

5. Why were the buffaloes important for the Indians?

   ....

6. How did the Indians lose their buffalo herds?

   ....

7. Why was the buffalo almost extinct by the end of the 19th century?

   ....

8. Why are the Hualapai lucky to own some of the land around the Grand Canyon?

   ....

Punkte: ☐ von 16

Lösungen Seite 118/119

Aufgabe 3 **Finde das entsprechende Wort im Englischen.**

1. Konflikt ....
2. Büffel ....
3. Siedler ....
4. Herde ....
5. überleben ....
6. Krankheit ....
7. Neuankömmling ....
8. Eisen ....

Punkte: ☐ von 8

Aufgabe 4 **Finde den Fehler und korrigiere ihn (Zusammenfassung).**

1. Katie started learning French four years ago and now she can French very well.

....

2. Mrs Johnson could not find the place they wanted to visit on the card.

....

3. It was happy the twins could visit the Skywalk for free.

....

4. The chieftain looked sadly when he told the twins how his tribe moved to the reservation.

....

5. When the Johnsons arrived at the reservation, they hadn't got something to eat.

....

6. After the settlers arrived, many Indians died on European illnesses.

....

Punkte: ☐ von 6

Punkte: ☐ von 40

34–40: Bravo! Beim Verstehen von Texten bist du dir schon sehr sicher.
20–33: Teilweise bist du sicher, teilweise noch nicht. Bearbeite bitte noch einmal die Übungen, in denen du beim ersten Mal viele Fehler hattest.
0–19: Leider ist dir noch zu vieles unklar. Arbeite das Kapitel bitte noch einmal durch.

Lösungen Seite 119

8 Wortschatz und Situationen

Learning words is boring? Well, maybe. But learning words can also be fun.
On the next pages you'll find some ideas to make learning words more interesting, exciting, a game with your friends ...
When you are learning words for school next time, just have a look at the following pages and use some of the ideas – and you'll see: learning words will be a lot easier.

8.1 Den Wortschatz sichern und erweitern

Alles klar?! **Wortfelder**

Mindmap

Wörter kannst du dir besser merken, wenn du sie im Zusammenhang mit anderen Wörtern lernst. Dafür eignet sich z. B. eine Mindmap oder Gedankenlandkarte, mit der du bestimmte Begriffe so anordnen kannst, dass die Zusammenhänge klar werden. Dafür schreibst du einen Begriff in die Mitte. Von diesem Begriff gehen dann Zweige und Äste ab, die die Struktur des Wortfeldes widerspiegeln.

Beispiel: Das Wortfeld TRAVEL

Übung 1 **In Johnsons Wohnmobil gibt es ganz viel, was die Familie in ihrem Haus hat, aber nicht alles. Ordne die einzelnen Möbel und anderen Dinge den Zimmern zu, in denen man die Dinge in der Regel findet. Manche Dinge, wie z. B. *curtains* oder *carpet*, gibt es natürlich in mehreren Zimmern.**

alarm clock armchair bathtub bed bin books bookshelves
carpet chair computer couch cupboard curtain desk desk lamp
dishwasher dressing table globe pillow poster
refrigerator shower sink table toilet paper TV set
wardrobe washbasin wastepaper basket water tap

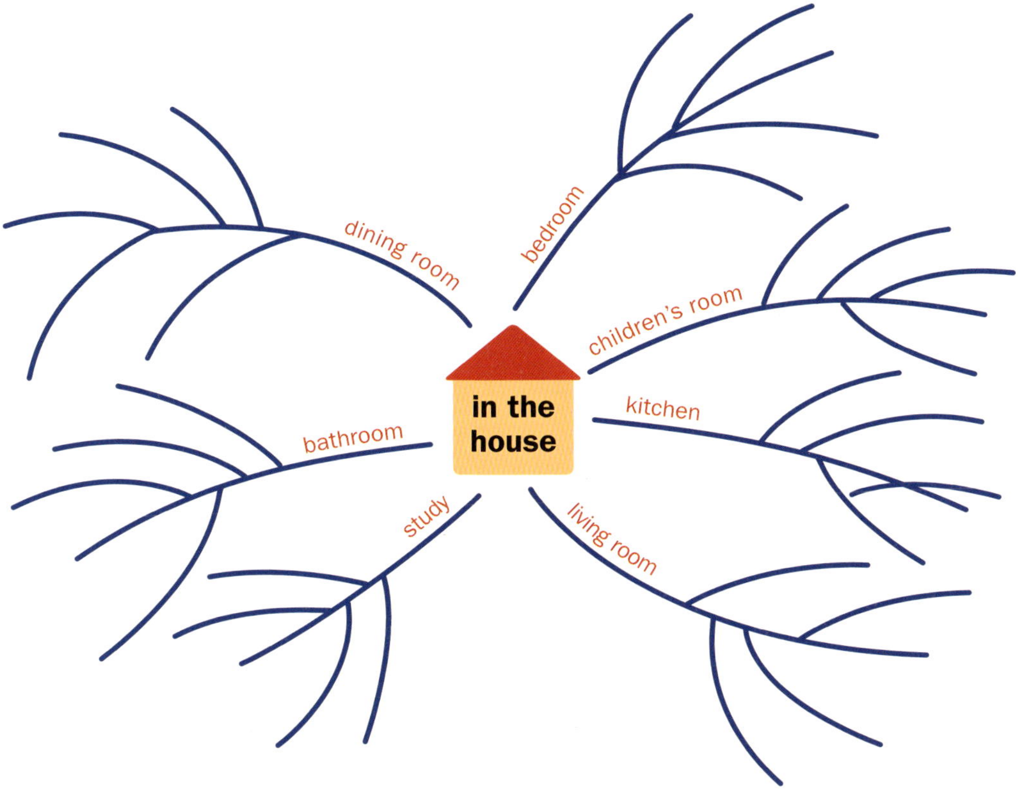

Alles klar?! **Spiele**

Den Wortschatz kannst du ganz gut üben, wenn du mit Freunden zusammen bist. Dann könnt ihr für euch Rätsel erstellen, die die anderen lösen, oder Spiele, die ihr gemeinsam spielt.

Crossword Puzzle

Erstelle ein Kreuzworträtsel. Und so gehst du vor:

- Suche dir einen kürzeren oder längeren Begriff, den du von oben nach unten schreibst, im Beispiel PLANE.
- Suche dir weitere Begriffe, die Buchstaben dieses Begriffs enthalten. Schreibe sie waagerecht an deinen senkrechten Begriff und mache daraus ein Kreuzworträtsel. Die Begriffe musst du natürlich herauslöschen, bevor du das Kreuzworträtsel deinem Freund oder deiner Freundin gibst. (Das wurde im Beispiel nicht gemacht, damit du siehst, wie es geht.)
- Überlege dir Fragen oder zeichne Bildchen, mit denen deine Freundin/dein Freund diese Begriffe erraten kann.

						6						
		1	C	A	M	**P**	E	R		V	A	N
2	T	R	A	V	E	**L**						
				3	C	**A**	R					
	4	T	R	A	I	**N**						
	5	G	U	I	D	**E**						

1 

2 To go from one place to another

3 

4 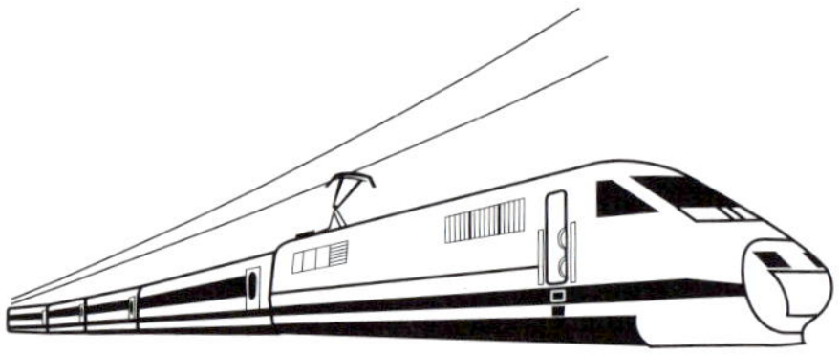

5 A person who shows sights to tourists

6 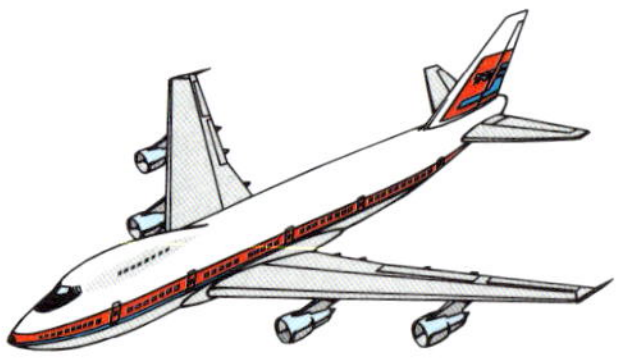

Remembering words

- Bastele zwei gleich große Kärtchen zu jeweils einem Wort. Auf das eine Kärtchen schreibst du das Wort, auf das andere malst du ein Bild oder schreibst die deutsche Übersetzung.
- Die Karten werden verdeckt hingelegt.
- Ihr spielt gemeinsam. Spieler A darf jeweils ein Kartenpaar aufdecken. Wenn die Karten zusammengehören, darf Spieler A das Kartenpaar behalten und ein weiteres Paar aufdecken, wenn nicht, kommt Spieler B an die Reihe.
- Wer am Ende die meisten Kartenpaare hat, hat gewonnen.

tent

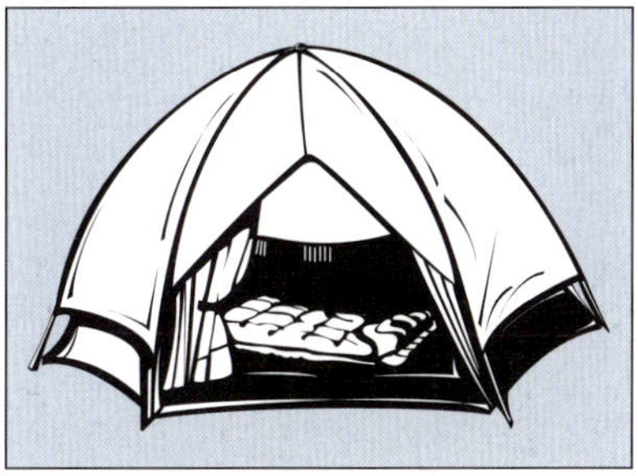

skyscrapers

campfire

Alles klar?! Richtig nachschlagen im Wörterbuch

Wörterbücher wie das „Power Dictionary" von Langenscheidt bieten dir viele praktische Hilfen, damit du das gesuchte Wort schnell findest.

100

child

C

child [tʃaɪld] ⚠ *Pl.*: **children** ['tʃɪldrən] Kind; ***be a good child!*** sei artig *oder* brav!; ***that's child's play*** *übertragen* das ist ein Kinderspiel
childbirth ['tʃaɪldbɜːθ] Geburt, Entbindung
childhood ['tʃaɪldhʊd] Kindheit; ***from childhood*** von Kindheit an
childish ['tʃaɪldɪʃ] **1.** kindlich **2.** *Erwachsener*: kindisch
childlike ['tʃaɪldlaɪk] kindlich
childminder ['tʃaɪld,maɪndə] *BE* Tagesmutter
childproof ['tʃaɪldpruːf] kindersicher; ***childproof lock*** *Auto*: Kindersicherung
children ['tʃɪldrən] *Pl. von* → ***child***; ***children's home*** Kinderheim
child seat ['tʃaɪld siːt] *Auto*: Kindersitz
chill¹ [tʃɪl] **1.** kühlen (*Getränk usw.*) **2.** ***chilled to the bone*** *Person*: (völlig) durchgefroren
chill² [tʃɪl] **1.** Erkältung; ***catch a chill*** sich erkälten **2.** Kälte (*auch übertragen*); ***take the chill off something*** etwas leicht anwärmen
chill³ [tʃɪl] *auch* ***chill out*** relaxen
chilly ['tʃɪlɪ] kalt, frostig (*auch übertragen*)
chime¹ [tʃaɪm] **1.** (Glocken)Schlag **2.** *oft* ***chimes*** *Pl.* Glockenspiel
chime² [tʃaɪm] **1.** (*Glocken*) läuten, (*Uhr*) schlagen
chimney ['tʃɪmnɪ] Schornstein, Kamin
chimney-piece ['tʃɪmnɪpiːs] Kaminsims
chimney-sweep ['tʃɪmnɪswiːp] Schornsteinfeger(in), Kaminkehrer(in)

chimpanzee [⚠ ,tʃɪmpæn'ziː] *umg. auch* ***chimp*** Schimpanse
chin [tʃɪn] **1.** Kinn **2.** (***keep your***) ***chin up!*** *umg.* Kopf hoch!, halt die Ohren steif!
China ['tʃaɪnə] China
china ['tʃaɪnə] **1.** Porzellan **2.** *auch* ***chinaware*** Porzellan(geschirr)
Chinatown ['tʃaɪnətaʊn] Chinatown, Chinesenviertel
Chinese¹ [,tʃaɪ'niːz] chinesisch
Chinese² [,tʃaɪ'niːz] *Sprache*: Chinesisch
Chinese³ [,tʃaɪ'niːz] Chinese, Chinesin; ***the Chinese*** *Pl.* die Chinesen
chink¹ [tʃɪŋk] Riss, Ritze, Spalt
chink² [tʃɪŋk] **1.** klirren, klimpern **2.** klirren *oder* klimpern mit
chinwag¹ ['tʃɪnwæg] *bes. BE, umg.* Plauderei, Plausch
chinwag² ['tʃɪnwæg] *bes. BE, umg.* plaudern, plauschen
chip¹ [tʃɪp] **1.** *an Tasse, Teller usw.*: angeschlagene Stelle **2.** *von Holz usw.*: Splitter, Span **3.** ***chips*** *Pl. BE* ⚠ Pommes frites **4.** ***chips*** *Pl. AE* ⚠ (Kartoffel)Chips **5.** *beim Roulette usw.*: Chip, Spielmarke **6.** *Elektrotechnik*: Chip

chips

Achte auf den Unterschied

Englisch	Deutsch
BE **chips**	Pommes frites
AE **(potato) chips**	Kartoffelchips

Deutsch	Englisch
Kartoffelchips	*BE* **crisps**, *AE* **(potato) chips**
Pommes frites	*BE* **chips**, *AE* **(French) fries**

Übrigens: Auch in britischen Restaurants werden Pommes frites oft als **French fries** bzw. **French fried potatoes** bezeichnet.

chip² [tʃɪp], ***chipped***, ***chipped*** anschlagen (*Geschirr usw.*)

chip in [,tʃɪp'ɪn] *umg.* **1.** *im Gespräch*: einwerfen (*Bemerkung usw.*) **2.** sich einmischen (*in ein Gespräch*) **3.** beisteuern (*Geld usw.*)
chip off [,tʃɪp'ɒf] abbrechen, abbröckeln

Übung 2 **Löse die folgenden Aufgaben mithilfe der Wörterbuchabbildung.**

<u>*When Tom was in London, he ate chips every day.*</u>

a) Schlage das Wort *chip* aus dem obigen Satz nach. (Die entsprechende Seite ist im „Langenscheidt Power Dictionary“ gegenüber schon aufgeschlagen.) Wo auf dieser Seite stehen die Informationen, die dir das Nachschlagen erleichtern, und wie lauten sie hier?

nach dem Stichwort | obere äußere Seitenecke | alphabetisch richtige Stelle | Seitenrand

Informationen	Wo stehen sie?	Wie lauten sie hier?
Buchstabe im Alphabet		
blaues Leitwort		
blaues Stichwort		
Hochzahl		

Mit so vielen Hilfen ist es doch ganz einfach, das Wort zu finden, das du suchst! Nun möchtest du ja aber auch noch wissen, was ***chips*** in dem Satz oben bedeutet – und die erste Übersetzung ist nicht immer die richtige Übersetzung! Moderne und gute Wörterbücher zeigen dir genau, in welchem Zusammenhang ein Wort vorkommen kann. Schau dir deshalb zu jeder Bedeutung (Ziffern 1. bis 6.) auch die *kursiven* Erklärungen an!

b) Schreibe hinter jede Zahl eine Bedeutung des Wortes **chip** aus dem Wörterbuch. Worauf kann sich die jeweilige Bedeutung beziehen? Fallen dir für „usw.“ noch andere Beispiele ein als die, die im Wörterbuch angegeben sind?

TIPP: Ein Warndreieck ⚠ bedeutet: „Vorsicht! Hier kann man etwas verwechseln!“

1. ....

2. ....

3. ....

4. ....

5. ....

6. ....

c) Wie heißt der Satz also auf Deutsch?

When Tom was in London, he ate chips every day.

....

Die Zeichnungen und der blaue Kasten im Wörterbuch zeigen dir nochmal ausführlich, was der Unterschied zwischen *chips* in Großbritannien und *chips* in den USA ist.

Lösungen Seite 120

8.2 Situationen meistern

Alles klar?! **Situations: Telephoning**

Für bestimmte Situationen ist es gut, wenn man nicht nur die Wörter weiß, sondern sich feststehende Wendungen merkt. Hier findest du sinnvoll Redemittel fürs Telefonieren.

Starting a call

A	B
Hello? It's Betty here. This is Betty. Is that Alan? Can I speak to Alan, please? I'm phoning because …	Hello, Alan Booth speaking. Oh, hello Betty.

Ending a call

I've got to go now.
It was nice talking to you.
I'll speak to you soon.
See you in the summer/next week/tomorrow/…
Thanks for phoning.
Bye!

Other useful vocabulary:

make a (phone) call · pick up the receiver · engaged tone · ringing tone · answer the phone · to hang up · cordless phone · mobile (phone) · to text · answering machine · to send a text message · public phone/pay phone/phone box · dialling code · cheap rate · telephone directory · charge

Achtung
Das Wort „Handy" ist eigentlich ein „deutsches" Wort. In Großbritannien heißt Handy *mobile (phone)*, in den USA *cell (phone)*.

Übung 1 **Lies den Text und versuche aus dem Kontext zu erschließen, was die fett gedruckten Wörter bedeuten. Schreibe die Bedeutung neben die Wörter unter dem Text.**

When the Johnsons planned their trip to the States they wanted to **make a phone call** to Alan Booth, Mrs Johnson's brother, who lives in Boston, to tell him that they were coming to the States in the summer. When they tried at eight o'clock there was a **ringing tone**, but nobody **picked up the receiver** so they thought that Alan was still at work. There was no **answering machine**, so they couldn't **leave a message**. When they tried at nine, there was the **engaged tone**, so they tried again a couple of minutes later and Alan **answered the phone**.
The Johnsons – like most families in Britain – have got a **cordless phone**. They passed the **handset** to all the family members so that everybody could say hello to uncle Alan. After their phone call they **hung up**.

1. to make a (phone) call ....
2. ringing tone ....
3. to pick up the receiver ....
4. answering machine ....
5. to leave a message ....
6. engaged tone ....
7. to answer the phone ....
8. cordless phone ....
9. handset ....
10. to hang up ....

Lösungen Seite 121

Übung 2 **Unterstreiche die Ausdrücke, die typisch für ein Telefongespräch sind.**

Tim: Hello, Tim Booth speaking.
Betty: Hello, Tim. This is Auntie Betty from Canterbury. How are you?
Tim: Oh, hello Auntie Betty. Fine, I'm just watching a great basketball match. Dallas Mavericks versus Boston Celtics. Boston is about to win.
Betty: I don't want to keep you. Can I speak to your Dad, please?
Tim: Sure. Dad, Dad … Auntie Betty is on the phone.
Alan: Hello, Betty. How are you?
Betty: We are fine. You know what – we are planning to do our big trip to the States this year … I'm phoning because …
Betty: Ok, that's settled. It was nice talking to you.
Alan: I'll speak to you soon. And see you in the summer. Thanks for phoning. Bye!
Betty: Bye.

Übung 3 **Bringe folgende Sätze in die richtige Reihenfolge, sodass ein sinnvolles Telefongespräch entsteht.**

Mandy: Bye.
Mandy: Hello, Canterbury 678912, Mandy Johnson speaking.
Mandy: I'm sorry she is not at home.
Mandy: Yes, of course.

Shop assistant: Can I leave a message? Can you tell her that she can pick up the book she ordered?
Shop assistant: High Street Book Shop. Can I speak to your mother, please?
Shop assistant: Thank you very much. Bye.

Mandy: ………………………………………………

Shop assistant: ………………………………………………

Mandy: ………………………………………………

Shop assistant: ………………………………………………

Mandy: ………………………………………………

Shop assistant: ………………………………………………

Mandy: ………………………………………………

Lösungen Seite 121

Übung 4 **Katie ruft ihre Freundin Clare an. Setze folgende Begriffe ein:**

Bye	Bye	Can I speak to	Hello	Hello	Hello	I'm phoning because
please	speaking	Thank you for calling	this is			

Paul: ...., Canterbury 789123, Paul Miller ....

Katie: ...., Paul, ... Katie. .... Clare, ...?

Paul: Sure, hang on a minute.

Clare: ...., Katie. What's up?

Katie: Not much. .... I wanted to ask if we're going riding tomorrow.

Clare: On no, sorry, I can't tomorrow. There is a maths test on Friday. I really have to work for that.

Katie: What a pity. Then I'll go by myself. Maybe next week some time?

Clare: Yeah, maybe. We'll talk about that on Friday. ....

Katie: ....

Übung 5 ★ **Ergänze die fehlenden Wendungen.**

Mark: ...., Canterbury 678912, Mark Johnson ....

Thomas: .... Thomas Green .... Thomas from football.

Mark: Oh, ..., Thomas. How are you?

Thomas: Fine, thanks. But .... I have a problem with the match on Saturday. James is ill and Emilia can't come either. Can you play?

Mark: Well, sure, yes. I'd like to. And you could also ask Mandy.

Thomas: That's what I wanted to do … ....

Mark: Yes, of course. Looking forward to Saturday. Bye. Mandy, Mandy …

Thomas: Bye …

Lösungen Seite 122

Abschlusstest (35 Minuten)

**STOPP!
Zuerst die Lernkärtchen durcharbeiten!**

Aufgabe 1 **Übersetze mithilfe deines Wörterbuchs.**

Englische Wörter haben oft mehrere Bedeutungen, deutsche aber auch. Und leider gibt es oft auch „falsche Freunde“.

Setze das richtige Wort für „Rezept“ ein:
Yesterday everything went wrong. First I tried out a new .... for a chocolate cake, but it tasted like sand. In the afternoon I went shopping for my mother. The weather was nice, so I walked all the way to the town centre. There I realized that I had forgotten my shopping list and the doctor's ....! Then it started to rain and by the time I got home I was dripping wet!

Und was bedeutet das englische Wort *receipt*? ....

Punkte: ☐ von 3

Aufgabe 2 **Übersetze. Du darfst gerne dein Wörterbuch benutzen.**

move

My mother was moved to tears.

....

Last year we moved to London.

....

Don't move!

....

Note

in der Musik: ....

in der Schule (British English): ....

in der Schule (American English): ....

Was heißt *note* (Nomen) außerdem? ....

Himmel

God lives in ....

Look at all the clouds in the ....

Punkte: ☐ von 9

Lösungen Seite 122

Aufgabe 3 **Stelle folgende Begriffe übersichtlich dar.**

bike	bus	car	motor bike	scooter	taxi
train	tram	underground	walk		

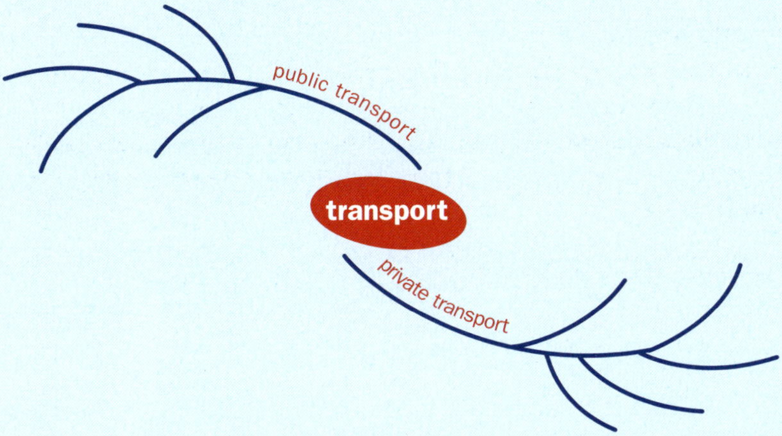

Punkte: ☐ von 10

Aufgabe 4 **Ordne zu.**

Bye! Can I speak to …, please? I'll speak to you soon.
I'm phoning because … I've got to go now. Is that …?
It was nice talking to you. It's … here. Hello?
See you tomorrow. Thanks for phoning. This is ….

Starting a call	**Ending a call**

Punkte: ☐ von 12

Lösungen Seite 123

Aufgabe 5 **Ergänze die fehlenden Wendungen.**

Mandy: ...., Canterbury 678912, Mandy Johnson ....

Andrew: ...., Mandy, ... Andrew. .... Katie, ...?

Mandy: Sure, hang on a minute.

Katie: ...., Andrew. What's up?

Andrew: Not much. .... I wanted to ask if we're going inline skating tomorrow afternoon.

Katie: Oh, that would be nice.

Andrew: What time can we meet?

Katie: Say four o'clock, in the park.

Andrew: Great. .... Bye.

Katie: .... Bye.

Punkte: ☐ von 10

Punkte: ☐ von 44

38–44: Bravo! Du weißt schon gut Bescheid.
23–37: Teilweise bist du sicher, teilweise noch nicht. Bearbeite bitte noch einmal die Übungen, in denen du beim ersten Mal viele Fehler hattest.
0–22: Leider ist dir noch zu vieles unklar. Arbeite das Kapitel bitte noch einmal durch.

Lösungen Seite 123

Lösungen

1.1 *Present Tense*/Präsens

Übung 1 (Seite 7)

1. The twins feed the cat every morning. Today Mandy is giving Maggie her food, because Mark is looking for his school things.
2. It is Friday afternoon and Katie is riding Little Richard. She usually rides him on Saturdays, but not this weekend as it is her mother's birthday.
3. Mrs Johnson often bakes a cake at the weekend. But today it is Katie and the twins who are baking two cakes for their mother's birthday.
4. Mandy and Mark have a judo lesson every Friday. This week they are practising a new throw which they are finding very difficult.
5. Mr Johnson likes to cycle to work every morning. But today it is raining hard so he is going by car.
6. Katie sometimes borrows a book from the library on her way home from school. She is now in the library and is looking for a book on horses.

Übung 2 (Seite 7)

1. The Johnsons go on holiday every year.
2. They often go on holiday in August.
3. They are planning their holiday in America.
4. They are sitting at the dining-table.
5. It is in the dining room.
6. No, she doesn't.
7. No, he doesn't.
8. They go on holiday.

1.2 *Future Tense*/Futur

Alles klar?! (Seite 8)

Signalwörter für *will-future*:

I think = ich denke
I hope = ich hoffe
perhaps = vielleicht

I suppose = ich nehme an, vermute
I'm sure = ich bin sicher
probably = vermutlich

next (week, month, year ...) = nächste Woche, nächsten Monat, nächstes Jahr ...
in (2050, three weeks ...) = im Jahr 2050, in drei Wochen ...
tomorrow = morgen

Übung 1 (Seite 9)

1. She is sure that her relatives will be nice.
2. She believes that her uncle will meet them at the airport.
3. She hopes that the plane will arrive on time.
4. She believes that she will not be travel sick.
5. She hopes that the flight will not take too long.
6. She is sure that her parents will hire a camper van.
7. She hopes that the weather will be fine in Boston.
8. She is sure that they will see many interesting places.
9. She believes that they will have a lot of fun.
10. She thinks that the family will enjoy the visit.

Übung 2 (Seite 10)

1. We have our tickets for the plane. We will see you at the airport.
2. We must leave now or we will miss the airport bus.
3. I think, we will enjoy our holiday in the USA.
4. Don't eat too much on the plane, Mark. You will be airsick.
5. I hope the weather will be fine in Boston.
6. Don't worry, we will take our umbrellas just in case.

Übung 3 (Seite 10)

1. It's rush hour. There will be a lot of traffic on the road to the airport.
2. Next week there is a public holiday in the USA. The Booths will come to Washington, too.
3. Wait, the red light is on. I will call the stewardess.
4. If the plane is late, Mr Booth will not wait at the airport.

Übung 4 (Seite 12)

1. The Johnsons are going to meet their parents at the airport after school.
2. They are going to fly to Boston for their holiday.
3. Our parents promised: we are going to hire a camper van.
4. The holiday is all planned. We are going to visit Boston, Washington and Philadelphia.
5. Look at the clouds! It is going to rain.
6. Katie has a brush in her hand. She is going to brush her horse.
7. Mrs Johnson called her brother on the phone. She is going to visit him in Boston.
8. The door of the plane is closing. The plane is going to take off.

Übung 5 (Seite 13)

1. Are you going to spend your holiday in Aviemore this year? – No, I'm not.
2. Will Grandma Booth brush my horse? – No, she won't. She's afraid of horses.
3. Will the weather be hot in Boston? – Yes, it will.
4. Are you going to fly to Boston at the weekend? – Yes, I am.
5. Will the flight take more than six hours? – Yes, it will.
6. Is your father going to hire a camper van in Boston? – Yes, he is.
7. Are you going to visit other cities in America? – Yes we are.
8. Will you sleep during the flight? – Yes, I will.
9. Will you send me a postcard from Boston? – Yes, I will.
10. Is your uncle going to meet your family at Boston Airport? – Yes, he is.

1.3 *Past Tense*/Vergangenheit

Übung 1 (Seite 14)

1. Katie got riding lessons for her birthday.
2. The twins joined the school orchestra.
3. The family visited the grandparents in London.
4. They went on a trip to the Tower of London.
5. They did not go on a boat trip on the Thames, because it was raining.

6. They saw the Changing of the Guard at Buckingham Palace.
7. Mrs Booth told the family about her son Alan in Boston.
8. Mr and Mrs Johnson decided to spend their next holiday in America.

Alles klar?! (Seite 15)

Bei der Bildung des *past participle* bei regelmäßigen Verben hängt man (wie bei der Bildung des *simple past*) an die Grundform des Verbs -ed an: *talked, asked*

- Verben, die auf einen Konsonanten + *y* enden: Das *y* wird zu i und du hängst -ed an.
- Verben, die mit einem stummen *-e* enden: Hier entfällt das e.
- Verben mit kurzem, einfachem Vokal, auf den ein Konsonant folgt: Der Konsonant wird verdoppelt.

write – written   do – done

Übung 2 (Seite 16)

1. Katie's horse is clean, she has just brushed it.
2. "Have you written a letter to Uncle Alan?" – "Yes, I have already finished it."
3. We have not been to America yet.
4. Katie has French at school. She has learned it for two years now.
5. The Booths have lived in Boston for three years.
6. Distances are so great in America. They have not visited New York yet.
7. Mrs Johnson has worked for the church for six years.
8. "Has Katie gone to her riding lesson?"– "Yes, she has already left."
9. The twins have fed the cat.
10. "Have the Johnsons booked their flights?" – "No, Mr Johnson has not phoned the travel agent yet."

Alles klar?! (Seite 17)

since + Zeitpunkt seit
for + Zeitraum seit
just gerade, soeben
not yet noch nicht
already schon

so far bisher, bislang, bis jetzt
ever jemals
up to now bisher, bislang, bis jetzt
never niemals
today/this morning/week (wenn dieser Zeitraum noch nicht vorbei ist) heute, heute Morgen, diese Woche

Übung 3 (Seite 18)

1. Mandy has just fed the cat.
2. Anne has never seen a French film.
3. The Booths have lived in Boston for three years.
4. We have already booked our flight to America.
5. The twins have not been to Washington yet.
6. Katie has had six riding lessons so far.
7. Have you ever flown in an aeroplane?
8. Maggie has caught six mice up to now.
9. Uncle Alan has never visited New York.
10. Mr Johnson has not driven a camper van yet.

Alles klar?! (Seite 19)

- Verben, die mit einem stummen -e enden: Hier entfällt das e.
- Verben mit kurzem, einfachem Vokal, auf den ein Konsonant folgt: Der Konsonant wird verdoppelt.
- Verben auf *-ie*: Das -ie wird zu einem -y.

Übung 4 (Seite 20)

On Sunday Katie was sitting at her desk when her mother came into the room. Katie was writing a letter to her Uncle Alan in Boston about the trip to the USA the family was planning. Katie and her mother were talking about their holiday when the phone rang. It was Uncle Alan. He asked about the time of their flight and said he hoped to meet them at the airport. Katie had a test in French at school the next day. She was learning for the test after supper, while the twins were playing monopoly. They were also very excited about the holiday; while they were playing monopoly they were listening to a programme about America on the radio.

Übung 5 (Seite 21)

It is Saturday afternoon and the Johnsons are all at home because it is raining. Katie is reading a book while Mark is doing his homework. He hopes that the rain will soon stop, because he and Ben are going to watch a football match in Canterbury. Mandy is talking to her mother about Uncle Alan. The Johnson children have not seen their uncle for a few years and they have never met his wife, Cindy. Mandy wants to know why her uncle went to America and how he met Aunt Cindy. Mrs Johnson says that he wanted to work in America to gain experience (= Erfahrung sammeln) as a computer expert. While he was looking for a job, he had an interview (= Einstellungsgespräch) with a firm where Cindy worked as a secretary. Six months later they were married (= verheiratet). "Do you think that Uncle Alan will ever come back to England to work?" Mandy asks. "I don't think so," her mother replies, "he earns much more money in America than he could ever earn in England."

Abschlusstest

Aufgabe 1 (Seite 22)

Tomorrow it will be cloudy in the morning and there will be heavy rain in the afternoon. In the evening our plane will leave for Boston. The flight will take nine hours and we will arrive early the next morning. Our relatives will meet us at the airport.

Aufgabe 2 (Seite 22)

1. Look, how grey the sky is! It is going to snow. (b)
2. We are going to visit Boston this summer. (a)
3. Uncle Alan is not going to meet us at the airport. His car has broken down. (b)
4. I'm tired of waiting. I am going to leave now. (a)

Aufgabe 3 (Seite 23)

Mrs J:	Where have you been, Katie? It's already time for supper.
Katie:	Sorry, I went to Anne's house. We had so much French homework that we forgot the time.
Mrs J:	What did you talk about, your horses?
Katie:	No, we discussed our holidays. Do you know that Anne has visited America? Have you seen New York, Mum?
Mrs J:	No, I have not visited America, but your father and I went to Scotland last year and we have seen many other countries so far.
Katie:	Oh, dear! And I have only explored London up to now.

Aufgabe 4 (Seite 23)

1. Have you ever visited America?
2. Have you not had breakfast so far?
3. Have you never seen your American cousin?
4. Have you already booked your flight?
5. Have you just entered the classroom?
6. Have you not yet done your homework?

Aufgabe 5 (Seite 24)

My name is Mary Booth, I have lived in Wimbledon all my life. My husband and I bought our house when we married and have lived in it for thirty years. We married in 1960 and we have two children. My daughter has lived in Canterbury for ten years and my son Alan moved to America three years ago. Since then, he has lived in Boston. While we were having supper last night, Alan phoned and told me that his sister and her family will visit him soon. He is going to meet them at the airport. During their visit they will make a trip to Washington and Philadelphia. It will be their first visit to America, but they have been to other countries in Europe and last year they went to Scotland.

2.1 *Modal Auxiliary Verbs*/Modale Hilfsverben

Übung 1 (Seite 27)

1. Yes, he could.
2. Yes, she can.
3. Yes, she can.
4. Yes, they can.
5. No, she couldn't.
6. Yes, he can.

Übung 2 (Seite 28)

1. Mandy: "Can I speak to Uncle Alan when he phones?" Bitte
2. Mrs Johnson: "Yes, you can, but don't speak for too long." Erlaubnis
3. Mark to his father: "I can't believe it. Mandy spoke to Uncle Alan for over a quarter of an hour." Unmöglichkeit
4. Mrs Johnson to Mandy: "You can't talk to Uncle Alan for so long next time. It is far too expensive." Verbot
5. Mandy: "But it was so interesting. Uncle Alan was telling me that when he first went to America, he couldn't always understand the way Americans speak English." Fähigkeit verneint
6. Mrs Johnson: "Your uncle is just too patient with you. Next time you have so many questions, you could tell him that you will write him an e-mail." Möglichkeit
7. Mandy: "I'm not going to write to him now. I can ask him everything I want to know when we reach Boston." Fähigkeit
8. Mrs Johnson: "Well that could take some time! Möglichkeit
   What a blessing that we can stay a few days with him and Aunt Cindy when we arrive next month." Zukünftiges

Übung 3 (Seite 29)

M & M: When can we go to Independence Hall?
Mrs J.: We can/could go today or tomorrow.
M & M: We can't go tomorrow, because Uncle Alan will be in Philadelphia and he wants to go inline skating with us. Can you and Dad come, too?
Mrs J.: You know that your father can't skate.
Mandy: But why can't he? I could skate when I was eight.
Mark: And I could skate when I was seven.
Mrs J.: Now, now you two. Your father has never learnt to skate. But you couldn't play the violin when you were five, could you?

Übung 4 (Seite 30)

1. No, she may not.
2. Yes, she may.
3. No, they may not.
4. Yes, they have.
5. No, they may not.
6. No, he may not.

Übung 5 (Seite 30)

For many years visitors to the Betsy Ross house have not been allowed to take photographs or use mobile phones. They may walk everywhere, but they mustn't touch the exhibits. Katie asks her father, "May we get nearer to the flag? I can't see it very well." "Yes, of course," her father says, "but not too close. You mustn't set the alarm off." Katie then asks her father, "May I take a photograph of the flag?" "No," he says, "you may not. When we leave, we will buy a postcard of the flag."

Übung 6 (Seite 32)

1. Which sights must the Johnsons see when they are in Philadelphia?
2. Visitors must leave the museum now. It closes in 10 minutes.
3. Mr Johnson needn't buy a postcard of the flag. His wife bought one yesterday.
4. Why did the Johnsons not have to leave the museum at 6 pm? Because on Saturday it was open until 9 pm.
5. You haven't eaten anything all day. You must be hungry.
6. Did you have to pay to see the Liberty Bell? No, I didn't. It is free.

Übung 7 (Seite 32)

Since 11th September 2001 Independence Hall und the Liberty Bell are in a security zone. Visitors must go through a security check. They must put their coats and bags in the cloakroom and they must pass through a special door, which checks for metal objects. The Johnsons had to wait half an hour at the security check, but they didn't have to show their tickets again. The attendant said, "You needn't show me your tickets. I checked them when you first came into the museum."

Abschlusstest

Aufgabe 1 (Seite 33)

1. We can go to the museum tomorrow.
2. Visitors may not/mustn't take photographs.
3. Mark could swim when he was seven.
4. Can we have an ice cream?
5. The Johnsons could see the Liberty Bell at 10 o'clock.
6. We have been able to see a lot of sights today.
7. They couldn't go to America last year.

Aufgabe 2 (Seite 33)

1. We must visit Independence Hall when we are in Philadelphia.
2. You needn't get to the museum before 9 o'clock, because it doesn't open until 9.15.
3. When the Johnsons reached the museum they had to put their coats and bags in the cloakroom.
4. Did Mr Johnson have to switch off his mobile phone? Yes, he did.
5. At the end of the day Mark asked, "Must we walk back to the camper van? I am so tired."
6. "No, we needn't walk. We can catch a bus."

Aufgabe 3 (Seite 34)

1. Can we have an ice cream? Yes, but you must eat it before we go to look at the Liberty Bell. Visitors mustn't eat anything in the Liberty Bell Center.
2. Mandy asks an attendant, "May we draw a picture of the Liberty Bell?" "Yes, you may/can, but you mustn't stop other visitors from seeing the bell. You must sit at the side of the room."
3. The Johnsons are sitting at the side of the room and Mark and Mandy are drawing a picture of the bell. Suddenly Mrs Johnson's mobile phone rings and she answers it. It is her brother. He wants to know, when the children can go inline skating. An attendant sees Mrs Johnson telephoning and tells her that she mustn't use her mobile phone in the Center. "But you needn't end your call," he says, "you can go outside to telephone."
4. Now Mrs Johnson is outside. She says to her brother, "They could go with you later today, but tomorrow is better." "Then we will go tomorrow," he replies.
5. That evening, Mrs Johnson tells her husband that she was very cross because she had to go outside the Center to telephone. "But it has been a lovely day and we have been able to see a lot of sights," she says.

3.1 *Indefinite Pronouns*/Indefinitpronomen

Übung 1 (Seite 36)

1. Katie has bought some postcards.
2. Mrs Booth is feeding some cats.
3. The twins have not got any shoes on.
4. There isn't any milk in the fridge.
5. Mark and Mandy have bought some cakes for tea.
6. Mr Johnson can't read the map, he is not wearing any glasses.

Übung 2 (Seite 37)

Katie: I am very hungry, Mum. Can I have something to eat, please?
Mark: I can't see Mandy anywhere, but I know she's in the van somewhere, because I can hear her.
Mark: Is there anybody there? I heard someone cough.
Mr J.: I can't find my sunglasses anywhere, may I have yours?
Mrs J.: No, you may not. I'm not going to lend you anything again, because you never give things back.

Übung 3 (Seite 38)

Mandy, listen! I think someone is outside the camper van.
Don't be silly, Mark. I can't hear anything.
Are you sure, Mandy? I definitely heard something.
No you didn't, Mark. There isn't anyone outside.
Has Uncle Alan said anything about a visit to New York yet, Mandy?
I think so, Mark. He said something to Dad at supper last night.
Oh dear, I can't find the guidebook for New York anywhere.
Well, it can't disappear. It must be somewhere in the van.
Does Uncle Alan know anyone in New York, Mandy?
I don't think so, Mark He hasn't said anything.
Isn't is fun! We have never done anything so exciting before.
We have never been anywhere as exciting as America before!

Übung 4 (Seite 39)

While the Johnsons were in New York they stayed in a small hotel. They got up early every day and had breakfast in a café only a few metres from their hotel. Everybody in the family was enjoying their trip to New York. They wanted to see everything of interest, go everywhere, but they had little time and they could only do a few things each/every day. They were really tired every evening when they went to bed, but after only a few hours of sleep they were ready to go anywhere.

Übung 5 (Seite 40)

1. There is nothing in the tank.
2. It is very early in the morning and there is nobody around to ask.
3. The streets are deserted (= leer), there is nobody/no one around.
4. Katie looks for the map (= Karte), but it is nowhere to be seen.
5. It was still early when they finally set off and it was so foggy (= neblig) that Mr Johnson could see nothing.

Übung 6 (Seite 41)

1. There isn't anything wrong.
2. No, I didn't see anybody.
3. I didn't do anything.
4. I didn't go anywhere.
5. I didn't ask anybody.
6. He didn't tell me anything.
7. You can't do anything.
8. It wasn't anywhere in the van.
9. I didn't pay him anything.
10. I didn't take it anywhere.

3.2 *Indefinite Numeral Adjectives*/Indefinite Zahladjektive

Übung 1 (Seite 42)

1. There was not much room in it for the family.
2. They were pleased to be in New York as there were a lot of things to do there.
3. They saw Times Square and Broadway and visited many museums.
4. They did not see Harlem as they did not have much time.
5. How many musicals did they see?
6. She spent too much money on postcards.

Übung 2 (Seite 43)

1. The Johnsons are spending a few days in New York.
2. She has not any plans for the evening.
3. They have seen many sights.
4. Katie only takes a little milk in her tea.
5. There were only few seats left in the theatre.
6. There were many/a lot of people in Times Square.
7. There was too little time to go to Harlem.
8. The twins did not have much sleep on the journey.

Abschlusstest

Aufgabe 1 (Seite 44)

some petrol
no petrol
a lot of petrol
little petrol

few relatives
some relatives
no relatives
many/a lot of relatives

a lot of time
little time
some time
no time

Aufgabe 2 (Seite 44)

1. I haven't got any coffee, but you can have some tea.
2. Mrs Johnson can't find her purse anywhere, but it must be somewhere in the camper van.
3. Mark is so lazy, he never does any work in the house.
4. Have you got any money with you in New York? Not here, but I've got some at home in Boston.
5. Can anyone in Washington speak French?
6. Anne can lend Katie some books about horses.
7. Katie hasn't got any books about horses yet.
8. There's something wrong with our camper van. Can Uncle Alan do anything about it?

Aufgabe 3 (Seite 45)

1. She doesn't want to see any friends.
2. She doesn't talk to anybody.
3. She doesn't go anywhere.
4. She doesn't do anything.
5. She doesn't want to see anybody.

Aufgabe 4 (Seite 45)

The twins must help to get things ready for the trip to New York because Uncle Alan has got only a little time today. There are many things on the list. They must buy a few apples and some oranges for the journey and some sugar and some coffee. They must also buy two bottles of milk, because there isn't any milk in the fridge in the camper van. Is there perhaps anything they have forgotten? Yes, they must also buy some maps in the bookshop. And where else must they go? They have thought of everything; they needn't go anywhere else. If the family get thirsty on the journey they can stop and buy a few bottles of coke or water as there will be nothing to drink in the fridge except milk.

Aufgabe 5 (Seite 46)

1. There is only a little milk left.
2. In the bag you will find a few apples left.
3. How many kilometres are on the clock?
4. I haven't got any petrol left in the tank.

Aufgabe 6 (Seite 46)

1. We need some milk.
2. I didn't see anybody in the street.
3. Can/could I have something to drink?
4. Did you see anything in Harlem?
5. Your sunglasses are somewhere in the camper van.
6. Did you eat a lot of cakes?

4.1 *Adjectives*/Adjektive

Alles klar?! (Seite 48)

- Prädikativer Gebrauch:

to be – sein
to become – werden
to get – werden
to grow – werden
to remain – bleiben
to seem – scheinen
to stay – bleiben

- Und: Verben der Sinneswahrnehmung

to look – aussehen
to feel – fühlen
to smell – riechen
to sound – sich anhören
to taste – schmecken

Übung 1 (Seite 49)

a tall tree
a happy boy
a green leaf
a sleepy cat
a red rose
a big bridge
a fast train
an old cable car

Übung 2 (Seite 49)

1. Katie's new dress looks nice.
2. Mandy is feeling happy.
3. Maggie has grown fat.
4. Mr Booth is getting old.
5. Mark's room is untidy.
6. This ice cream tastes nice.

Übung 3 (Seite 51)

high, higher, highest
nice, nicer, nicest
easy, easier, easiest
big, bigger, biggest
expensive, more expensive, most expensive
interesting, more interesting, most interesting
exciting, more exciting, most exciting
beautiful, more beautiful, most beautiful
simple, simpler, simplest
sad, sadder, saddest

Übung 4 (Seite 51)

1. It is a hot day today. It is hotter than yesterday.
2. It is often foggy in San Francisco. It is the foggiest place in California.
3. New York is very cold in winter. It is colder than San Francisco.
4. New York is an exciting city, but it is not as exciting as San Francisco.
5. There is a fast train to New York, but it is faster to go by plane.
6. Mandy has just watched a sad film. It was the saddest film she has ever seen.
7. The Eiffel Tower is tall, but the Empire State Building is taller.
8. Katie is a good horse rider, but Anne is better than her.
9. French lessons are interesting. They are more interesting than maths lessons.
10. Ben is a bad football player. He is the worst player in the team.

4.2 *Adverbs*/Adverbien

Alles klar?! (Seite 52)

Adverbien, die die Form von Adjektiven haben:

early – früh
fast – schnell
high – hoch
long – lang
low – niedrig

Übung 1 (Seite 53)

1. Mandy and Mark are eagerly looking forward to the trip to Alcatraz Island.
2. They run quickly to the boat.
3. The boat crosses San Francisco Bay slowly, because there are many other boats nearby.
4. The captain steers the boat carefully round the rocks.
5. He speaks clearly so that the passengers can easily hear what he says about the murderers in Alcatraz prison.
6. Luckily, Mandy and Mark do not feel frightened by the captain's stories.
7. When the boat returns to San Francisco, they are terribly hungry.
8. "Did you enjoy the trip?" Mrs Johnson asks the twins. "Oh yes, it was really exciting."

Übung 2 (Seite 53)

1. Anne does not let her horse jump over high fences. (Adj.)
2. Mark threw the ball up high. (Adv.)
3. Mark does not like to get up early. (Adv.)
4. Katie likes to take the early bus to school. (Adj.)
5. Yesterday she did not take long to do her homework. (Adv.)
6. It was a long journey for the Johnsons from New York to San Francisco. (Adj.)
7. It's better to take the fast train. (Adj.)
8. Mark and Mandy had to run fast to catch the boat. (Adv.)

Übung 3 (Seite 54)

1. Ben lives near Mark.
2. Katie could hardly see the first American flag in the Betsy Ross house.
3. Mr Johnson has read a lot of books on earthquakes lately.
4. Katie and Anne have nearly finished their homework.
5. Mandy was angry with Mark, because they were late for school.
6. Mark does not work very hard.

Alles klar?! (Seite 54)

Beispiele für unregelmäßige Formen, die du lernen musst:

well – better – best: gut – besser – am besten
badly – worse – worst: schlecht – schlechter – am schlechtesten

Übung 4 (Seite 54)

1. When the bus reached Golden Gate Bridge, it drove more slowly.
2. Cable cars do not travel faster than buses.
3. Cars can travel fastest on motorways.
4. Ben plays football worst when he is the goalkeeper.
5. He plays better when he is a defender (= Verteidiger).
6. Mark plays best when he can score a goal.

Abschlusstest

Aufgabe 1 (Seite 55)

1. Mandy gets angry (P) when Mark is late (P).
2. The Redwoods are the tallest (A) living things on earth.
3. Golden Gate Bridge is the longest (A) bridge the Johnsons have ever seen.
4. Mandy asks her father, "Is there a longer (A) bridge anywhere in the world?"
5. There are not many old (A) buildings in San Francisco, because the terrible (A) earthquake in 1906 destroyed (= zerstören) most of them.
6. Have you heard the latest (A) news about the forest fires? Yes, it sounds awful (P).

Aufgabe 2 (Seite 55)

Mrs Johnson has been to see the Californian Redwoods. These trees grow very old and very tall. The oldest can live for over 2,000 years and the tallest can reach 115 metres high. Mrs Johnson got up early to catch the bus to the Redwood State Park. The bus drove fast along the coastal highway, but it was still a long journey. When they arrived Mrs Johnson walked round the park and felt very happy to see the beautiful trees. On the journey back the bus had to take a longer route, because of forest fires. Mrs Johnson remained quite calm. Later that evening she said to her husband, "The trees looked really spectacular. What a pity that you didn't come, too."

Aufgabe 3 (Seite 56)

Mr Johnson is reading about the earthquake in 1906. It was one of the most destructive natural disasters ever, but the fire that followed was even worse. It was more frightening for the people of San Francisco than the earthquake, because they had less water than they needed to extinguish it. The most terrible thing was that nearly everyone lost their home. Today an earthquake is more likely to occur in the San Francisco area than in the rest of America.

Aufgabe 4 (Seite 56)

1. Katie is a careful rider. She rides carefully.
2. Mr Johnson is a fast cyclist. He cycles fast.
3. Anne is a good rider. She rides well.
4. Mrs Johnson is a hard worker. She works hard.
5. Ben is a bad football player. He plays badly.
6. Mandy is a beautiful singer. She sings beautifully.

5.1 *Conditional Clauses (If-Clauses)*/Konditionalsätze (Typ I)

Alles klar?! (Seite 58)

*If you **come** to California,*	you ***will have*** a great holiday.
present tense	*will-future*

Übung 1 (Seite 59)

1. If the Johnsons want to see California, they will need a camper van.
2. If they visit Santa Barbara, they will see many Spanish-type houses.
3. If Katie goes to Hollywood, she will take a bus.
4. Uncle Alan will catch the train into Boston at 8 am, if he leaves now.
5. If Mark eats too many biscuits in the van, he will feel sick.
6. The Johnsons will spend the night in Carmel, if they find a camping site.
7. They will remember Clint Eastwood, if they stop in Carmel.
8. They will see many seals, if they take the Pacific coastal road.

Übung 2 (Seite 59)

1. If Katie stays longer, she will miss the Hollywood bus.
2. If the twins go to bed at 10 pm, they will be tired next morning.
3. If the Johnsons have enough time, they will spend two days in L.A.
4. If Mr Johnson tells Mrs Johnson the cost of the van, she will be angry.

Übung 3 (Seite 60)

1. when
2. if
3. if
4. when
5. if
6. when

Übung 4 (Seite 61)

You will not enjoy the trip if you get car sick.
You will not have time for the Grand Canyon if you stay too long in Yosemite.
You will not see the sunset over the Pacific if you do not stay awake.
You will miss the plane if you do not get to the airport on time.

5.2 *Relative Clauses*/Relativsätze

Übung 1 (Seite 62)

1. A camper van is a vehicle which is large.	which
2. Mrs Booth, who lives in London, is Katie's grandmother.	who
3. California is a state which has a lot of sunshine.	which
4. Mark, who is a twin, looks just like his sister Mandy.	who
5. This is the camping site that is cheapest.	that
6. People who live in California are called Californians.	who
7. Uncle Alan is the man whose home is in Boston.	whose
8. Katie is the girl whose friend has a horse.	whose

Übung 2 (Seite 63)

1. Alan Booth is a person who has a sister in Canterbury.
2. A camper van is a vehicle which needs a lot of petrol.
3. Katie is a girl who loves horses.
4. Travelling by camper van is a way of having a holiday which is cheap.
5. Hollywood is a place which is famous for its film stars.
6. An author is someone who writes books.

5.3 *Question Tags*/ „Frageanhängsel“

Alles klar?! (Seite 64)

She ***took*** *many photos,* ***didn't she****?*
bejaht verneint

She ***didn't take*** *many photos,* ***did she****?*
verneint bejaht

Übung 1 (Seite 64)

1. Katie took this photo of Yosemite National Park, didn't she?
2. Mr and Mrs Johnson will spend two days in the Grand Canyon, won't they?
3. They won't visit Las Vegas, will they?
4. The twins didn't visit Hollywood, did they?
5. You really will fill the tank with petrol, won't you?
6. Santa Barbara is not very far from L.A., is it?
7. San Francisco is a really beautiful city, isn't it?
8. You won't forget to send Uncle Alan a card, will you?
9. The twins have got many friends, haven't they?
10. Katie doesn't drive the camper van, does she?

Abschlusstest

Aufgabe 1 (Seite 65)

1. If Katie walks faster, she will not get wet.
2. If we leave now, we will be in L.A. at midday.
3. If we go to the Grand Canyon, we will see bears.
4. Katie will be a good horse rider if she practises more.
5. If you wait for me, Mark, I will help you do the washing up.
6. Mandy will post a card to her friend at home if she finds a post-box.

Aufgabe 2 (Seite 65)

1. Mrs Booth is the lady whose son lives in Boston
2. Avis is the company which provided the camper van.
3. Katie, is this your jacket which/that is lying on the floor?
4. Is Mr Johnson the man who hired the camper van?
5. Alan Booth is the man whose family is visiting from England.
6. Look at the man who is climbing the mountain in Yosemite.

Aufgabe 3 (Seite 66)

1. Uncle Alan will be at the airport when our plane from L. A. lands.
2. Katie will take a photograph if she sees a bear in the park.
3. Mark and Mandy want to see the dolphins when they visit San Diego.
4. Mr and Mrs Johnson will go walking in Yosemite if they have time.

Aufgabe 4 (Seite 66)

1. You will help me, won't you?
2. If you clean the fridge, I will cook lunch.
3. Katie is the girl, who likes riding.
4. Mark and Mandy are the children, whose uncle lives in Boston.
5. The Johnsons had a lovely holiday in America, didn't they?
6. Katie is interested in cinema films, isn't she?

6.1 *Adverbials*/Adverbiale

Übung 1 (Seite 68)

The Johnsons are now driving to the Indian reservation. Mark and Mandy are tired and Mandy asks, "When will we get there?" Her mother replies, "We'll be there soon." But the road never seems to end. "Have we ever been on a road that is as bumpy as this?" Mark asks. "No, never," Katie says. "That's not quite true," their father answers. "We often drive along bumpy roads in England, but this camper van is very old and so we can feel every bump."
At last Mrs Johnson sees the sign to the reservation; they have only 10 kilometres to go. After they have turned left and then right, they reach the Hualapai reservation. Everyone is very pleased that the journey is over.

Übung 2 (Seite 69)

Mrs Johnson has written a card to her brother Alan in Boston. This is what she wrote:
We were wrong; the journey was not really over. We had to walk almost vertically for one kilometre down a very steep path to the village. As we had all our bags with us, we could only walk very slowly. We finally reached the village in the evening and we were by now all very hungry. We immediately started to look for somewhere to eat, but there wasn't a restaurant anywhere. Luckily an Indian family saw us and asked, "Can we help you?" I quickly told them how hungry we were. "Sadly, we don't have any restaurants here," they said. "But if you come with us, we will gladly give you something to eat." We followed the kind Indians to their house. There we hungrily ate a delicious meal and happily accepted their invitation to stay the night after we learnt that we needed a tent to sleep in, which we had unfortunately forgotten.

Übung 3 (Seite 70)

1. It means "People of the Tall Pines".
2. They live on a reservation.
3. They believe that it began at "Spirit Mountain".
4. The number of people in the tribe is 1,532.
5. They work in the tourism industry and in cattle ranching.
6. They work in the tourism industry and in the tribe's arts and crafts shops.

6.2 *Adverbial Clauses*/Adverbialsätze

Übung 1 (Seite 71)

Mark and Mandy want to see the Grand Canyon from the glass Skywalk, because they hope that it will be very exciting to stand on the thick glass floor, which juts out 20 metres, and look down at the Canyon (kausal). Some visitors are quite afraid and desperately hold on to the glass walls. The twins are sure that they will walk fearlessly across the Skywalk if their parents will take them to see it (konditional). Mr Johnson does not really want to go to the Skywalk because he thinks that it will be very expensive (kausal).

Übung 2 (Seite 72)

1. Why did Mr Johnson drive slowly?
2. When did the Johnsons reach the village?
3. Where did the Johnsons have a delicious meal?
4. When did Mrs Johnson reserve the horses?
5. Why do the twins want to go the Skywalk?
6. Why doesn't Mr Johnson want to go to the Skywalk?

Übung 3 (Seite 72)

1. The Johnson children got very tired, because it was a long journey to the reservation.
2. The Johnsons were all very hungry when they finally reached the village.
3. As soon as they arrived, they started looking for somewhere to eat.
4. The Johnsons thought that they could hire a tent until the Indian family told them that visitors have to bring one with them.
5. Early in the morning before the rest of the family woke up, Mrs Johnson reserved two horses for Katie and herself to go riding the whole day.
6. After it stopped raining, they went riding.

Übung 4 (Seite 73)

Mrs Johnson reserved two horses as soon as she woke up.
Mandy is going to write another postcard to her uncle before she flies back to England.
The twins are sure that they will be able to learn a lot about Indian culture if their friends have time to show them round the village.
Mr Johnson made sure that the twins had something to do before he went fishing.
Mark wants to find out how Indians used to hunt while he is staying at the reservation.
Katie wants to buy a bracelet (= Armband) from the arts and crafts shop if she can find one that is not too expensive.
The twins will be very disappointed if they cannot go to the Skywalk.
Mrs Johnson is cross with her husband because he doesn't want to pay for the family to visit the Skywalk.
Katie is looking forward to riding Little Richard again when she returns home.
Mrs Johnson and Katie want to ride the horses where the Canyon is not too steep.

Abschlusstest

Aufgabe 1 (Seite 74)

1. When they arrived at the Indian village in the evening, they were very tired.
2. The next morning Katie and the twins did not wake up very early.
3. Mrs Johnson reserved two horses for Katie and herself to go riding the whole day.
4. Mr Johnson promised the twins that they could visit the Skywalk the next day, if it wasn't too expensive.
5. He said to them, "I want to go fishing in the afternoon. What are you going to do?"
6. "Our Indian friends, Don and Tobey, are going to show us the village, and we will see how Indians lived in the past and how they live today."

Aufgabe 2 (Seite 74/75)

Don and Tobey have kindly given the twins a photo album to look at, in which they can see pictures of an Indian powwow. Traditionally, this is a meeting of Indian tribes where the chieftains talk about important things in the biggest wigman and the tribes celebrate Indian culture by singing and dancing. Mark and Mandy are looking excitedly at all the photos, because Indian life really interests them. The twins can see that some Indians are dancing with great enthusiasm and that others are talking and singing. The brightly coloured costumes, which are beautifully decorated with feathers and beads, fascinate them most of all. "We are having a powwow next week," Don tells the twins. "Can you stay until then?" "Oh no", Mark says sadly, "we are flying to Boston on Friday". "Well, perhaps we could take you to meet our chieftain instead," Tobey says. The twins are thrilled and accept happily.

Aufgabe 3 (Seite 75)

1. They see the pictures in a photo album.
2. Because Indian life really interests them.
3. They talk about important things in the biggest wigwam.
4. They celebrate their culture by singing and dancing.
5. They dance with great enthusiasm.
6. They are flying to Boston on Friday.

Aufgabe 4 (Seite 76)

1. The Indian costumes were beautifully decorated.
2. Sadly, the twins are going to miss the powwow, but they are now luckily able to visit the Skywalk.
3. The Hualapai chieftain kindly invited the twins to visit the Skywalk for free.
4. Unhappily, the twins forgot to take a photo of the chieftain.
5. Mr and Mrs Johnson wisely got up early to pack their bags.

7.1 Reading and Understanding/Lesen und Verstehen

Übung 1 (Seite 78)

The Indians had lived in America for thousands of years when the Europeans started to arrive in the 17th century. At that time there were about 12 million Indians living there in more than one thousand different tribes.
At first the Indians welcomed the settlers enthusiastically. They found their white faces, their unusual clothes and their fine ships fascinating as well as the many things the settlers brought with them to start a new life.
In the early days the settlers found it difficult to grow food in the 'New World' and it was often the Indians who helped them to survive. But as time went on, conflicts began to develop between the Native Americans and the newcomers. The main reason for the wars that followed was the fight for land. The settlers wanted to own the land and use it themselves. They did not want to allow the Indians to graze their animals and grow crops on it anymore. The Indians, for their part, wanted to live in harmony with nature and they did not like the way the settlers made money out of the land and all it produced, like the buffalo, the trees, and the coal and iron deposits.
Many of the Native Americans died from the European illnesses which the settlers brought with them. Those who survived were not able to defend their lands against the large numbers of settlers, who fought in a well-organised army. The newcomers steadily drove the Indians from one place to another and took more and more of their lands for farming. With the loss of their lands many tribes also lost their large buffalo herds, which used to roam the prairie and provide the Indians with food, clothing and other things they needed. The settlers did not look after the buffalo, which were now on their lands, but killed them to sell their hides. By the end of the 19th century the buffalo were almost extinct.
In the end, the United States government gave land to each of the Indian tribes: the Indian Reservations. But the land was often very poor and the Indians could not grow much food on it. This was a situation that made all Indians very sad. Today, there are one or more Indian reservations in every state. The Hualapai, in the end, is lucky to own the rocky land around a part of the Grand Canyon. People from all over the world visit this beautiful place and happily pay to walk on the new Skywalk, which, in a way, is the Hualapai's 'new buffalo'.

Übung 2 (Seite 79)

Conflicts began to develop when the settlers, who did not want to allow the Native Americans to graze their animals and grow crops on their land anymore, drove the Indians off the land. With the loss of their lands many tribes also lost their large buffalo herds that provided them with food, clothing and other things they needed. Many of the Indians died from European illnesses which the settlers brought with them and weren't able to defend their land anymore. The government gave land to each of the Indian tribes on so- called Reservations, which was often very poor land and hard to grow food on. Tribes like the Hualapai, who are lucky to own a part of the beautiful land around the Grand Canyon, get money from people that visit their land.

Übung 3 (Seite 79)

settler (Z. 4):	Siedler	to survive (Z. 8):	überleben
conflict (Z. 8):	Konflikt	to develop (Z. 9):	entwickeln
fight (Z. 10):	Kampf	to own (Z. 10):	besitzen
to graze (Z. 11):	weiden lassen	crops (Z. 11):	Feldfrüchte
buffalo (Z. 13):	Büffel	newcomer (Z. 9):	Neuankömmling
deposit (Z. 14):	Lager(stätte)	iron (Z. 14):	Eisen
illness (Z. 15):	Krankheit	to defend (Z. 16):	verteidigen
herd (Z. 19):	Herde	to roam (Z. 20):	umherstreifen, wandern

Übung 4 (Seite 80)

1. enthusiasm	enthusiastic	5. sadness	sad
2. fascination	fascinating	6. luck	lucky
3. difficulty	difficult	7. rock	rocky
4. illness	ill	8. happiness	happy

Übung 5 (Seite 80)

1. white	black	5. poor	rich
2. difficult	easy	6. lucky	unlucky
3. good	bad	7. ugly	beautiful
4. large	small		

Übung 6 (Seite 80)

1. The settlers' white faces, their unusual clothes, their fine ships and all the things they brought with them fascinated the Indians.
2. Conflicts developed between the Indians and the settlers because the settlers wanted to own the land on which the Indians grew their crops and grazed their animals.
3. The Indians didn't like the way the settlers made money out of the land and what it produced.
4. Many Indians died because of the illnesses the Europeans brought with them.
5. The settlers were able to take away the Indians' land because they had a well-organised army and there were not enough Indians left to defend it.
6. The American government gave the Indians land to live on.
7. The Skywalk is called the Hualapai's 'new buffalo' because it provides them with money to buy food, clothing and all the other things they need.

Abschlusstest

Aufgabe 1 (Seite 81)

1. settler	to settle	6. fight	to fight
2. loss	to lose	7. owner	to own
3. life	to live	8. production	to produce
4. growth	to grow	9. death	to die
5. development	to develop	10. visitor	to visit

Aufgabe 2 (Seite 81)

1. The Indians had lived in America for thousands of years.
2. 12,000 Indians lived in each tribe on average.
3. The Indians helped the settlers to grow food.
4. The settlers didn't want the Indians to graze their animals and grow crops on the land anymore.
5. The buffaloes provided the Indians with food, clothing and other things they needed.
6. The Indians lost their buffalo herds because the settlers now owned the lands on which the buffalo roamed.

7. The buffalo was almost extinct because the settlers didn't look after them, but killed them to sell their hides.
8. The Hualapai are lucky to own this land because it is very beautiful and people who visit it from all over the world are happy to pay to walk on the Skywalk.

Aufgabe 3 (Seite 82)

1. Konflikt	conflict	5. überleben	to survive
2. Büffel	buffalo	6. Krankheit	illness
3. Siedler	settler	7. Neuankömmling	newcomer
4. Herde	herd	8. Eisen	iron

Aufgabe 4 (Seite 82)

1. Katie started learning French four years ago and now she can speak French very well.
2. Mrs Johnson could not find the place they wanted to visit on the map.
3. It was lucky the twins could visit the Skywalk for free.
4. The chieftain looked sad when he told the twins how his tribe moved to the reservation.
5. When the Johnsons arrived at the reservation, they hadn't got anything to eat.
6. After the settlers arrived, many Indians died of European illnesses.

8.1 Den Wortschatz sichern und erweitern

Übung 1 (Seite 85)

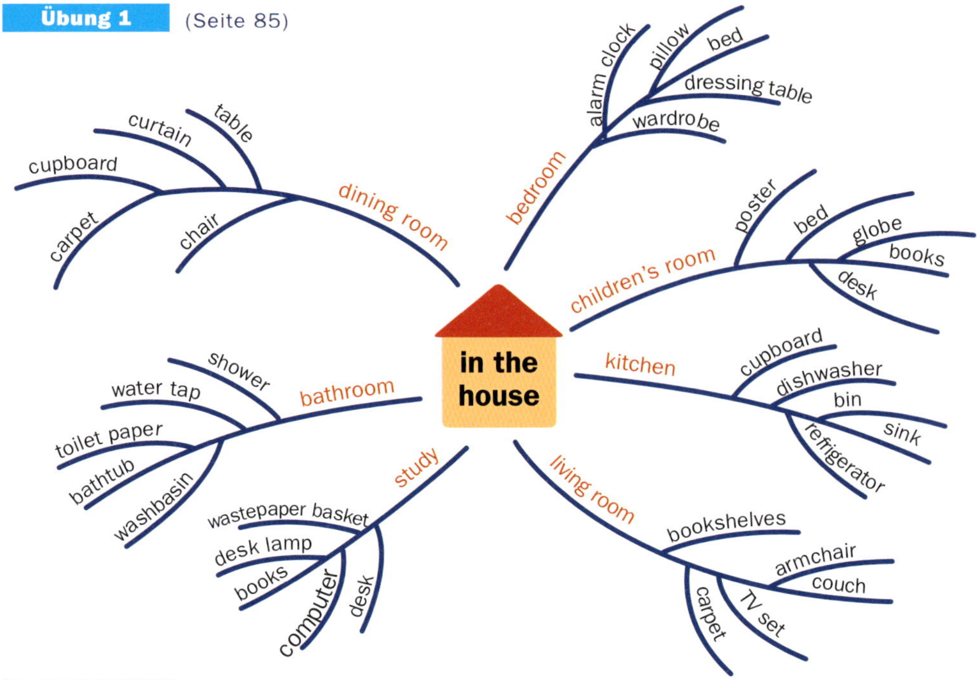

Übung 2 (Seite 89)

a)

Informationen	**Wo stehen sie?**	**Wie heißen sie hier?**
Buchstabe im Alphabet	Seitenrand	C
blaues Leitwort	obere, äußere Seitenecke	child
blaues Stichwort	alphabetisch richtige Stelle	chip
Hochzahl	nach dem Stichwort	1

b) 1. angeschlagene Stelle (z. B. an Tasse, Teller, aber auch: an Vase, Becher, Waschbecken)
2. Splitter, Span (z. B. an einem Stück Holz, aber auch: an Porzellan, Glas, Schokolade)
3. Pommes frites – aber nur im britischen Englisch! (Pl. BE = Plural, British English)
4. (Kartoffel-)Chips – aber nur im amerikanischen Englisch! (Pl. AE = Plural, American English)
5. Spielmarke, Chip (z. B. beim Roulette, aber auch: beim Brettspiel, für Spielautomaten)
6. Chip (in der Elektrotechnik, z. B. Mikrochip beim Computer, Speicherchip der Digitalkamera)

c) When Tom was in London, he ate chips every day.
Als Tom in London war, hat er jeden Tag Pommes frites gegessen.

8.2. Situationen meistern

Übung 1 (Seite 91)

1. to make a (phone) call — einen Telefonanruf machen
2. ringing tone — Freizeichen
3. to pick up the receiver — den Hörer abnehmen
4. answering machine — Anrufbeantworter
5. to leave a message — eine Nachricht hinterlassen
6. engaged tone — Besetztzeichen
7. to answer the phone — ans Telefon gehen
8. cordless phone — schnurloses Telefon
9. handset — Mobilteil
10. to hang up — auflegen

Übung 2 (Seite 92)

Tim: Hello, Tim Booth speaking.
Betty: Hello, Tim. This is Auntie Betty from Canterbury. How are you?
Tim: Oh, hello Auntie Betty. Fine, I'm just watching a great basketball match. Dallas Mavericks versus Boston Celtics. Boston is about to win.
Betty: I don't want to keep you. Can I speak to your Dad, please?
Tim: Sure. Dad, Dad … Auntie Betty is on the phone.
Alan: Hello, Betty. How are you?
Betty: We are fine. You know what – we are planning to do our big trip to the States this year … I'm phoning because …

Betty: Ok, that's settled. It was nice talking to you.
Alan: I'll speak to you soon. And see you in the summer. Thanks for phoning. Bye!
Betty: Bye.

Übung 3 (Seite 92)

Mandy: Hello, Canterbury 678912, Mandy Johnson speaking.
Shop assistant: High Street Book Shop. Can I speak to your mother, please?
Mandy: I'm sorry she is not at home.
Shop assistant: Can I leave a message? Can you tell her that she can pick up the book she ordered.
Mandy: Yes, of course.
Shop assistant: Thank you very much. Bye.
Mandy: Bye.

Übung 4 (Seite 93)

Paul: Hello, Canterbury 789123, Paul Miller speaking.
Katie: Hello, Paul, this is Katie. Can I speak to Clare, please?
Paul: Sure, hang on a minute.

Clare: Hello, Katie. What's up?
Katie: Not much. I'm phoning because I wanted to ask if we're going riding tomorrow.
Clare: On no, sorry, I can't tomorrow. There is a maths test on Friday. I really have to work for that.
Katie: What a pity. Then I'll go by myself. Maybe next week some time?
Clare: Yeah, maybe. We'll talk about that on Friday. Thank you for calling. Bye.
Katie: Bye.

Übung 5 (Seite 93)

Mark: Hello, Canterbury 678912, Mark Johnson speaking.
Thomas: Hello. It's Thomas Green here. Thomas from football.
Mark: Oh, hello, Thomas. How are you?
Thomas: Fine, thanks. But I'm phoning because I have a problem with the match on Saturday. James is ill and Emilia can't come either. Can you play?
Mark: Well, sure, yes. I'd like to. And you could also ask Mandy.
Thomas: That's what I wanted to do … Can I speak to her, please?
Mark: Yes, of course. Looking forward to Saturday. Bye. Mandy, Mandy …
Thomas: Bye …

Abschlusstest

Aufgabe 1 (Seite 94)

recipe
prescription
Quittung, Beleg

Aufgabe 2 (Seite 94)

move
Meine Mutter war zu Tränen gerührt.
Letztes Jahr zogen wir nach London.
Keine Bewegung!

Note
in der Musik: note
in der Schule (British Englisch): mark
in der Schule (American Englisch): grade
note bedeutet außerdem: Notiz, Anmerkung (auf Buchseite), Zettel (mit kurzer Notiz), Geldschein (BE)

Himmel
God lives in Heaven.
Look at all the clouds in the sky.

Aufgabe 3 (Seite 95)

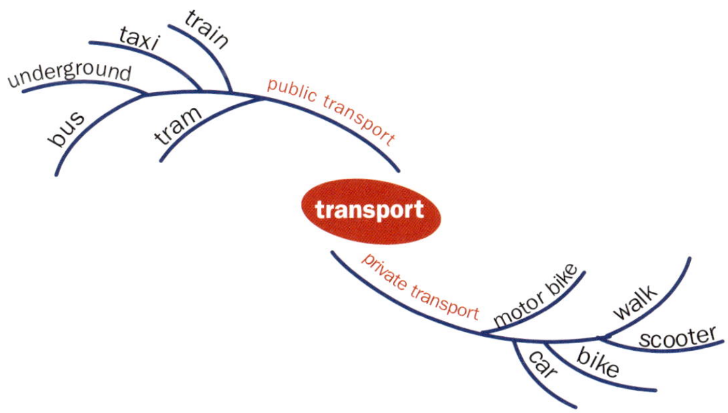

Aufgabe 4 (Seite 95)

Starting a call	Ending a call
Hello? It's … here. This is … . Is that …? Can I speak to …, please? I'm phoning because …	I've got to go now. It was nice talking to you. I'll speak to you soon. See you tomorrow. Thanks for phoning. Bye!

Aufgabe 5 (Seite 96)

Mandy: Hello, Canterbury 678912, Mandy Johnson speaking.
Andrew: Hello, Mandy, this is Andrew. Can I speak to Katie, please?
Mandy: Sure, hang on a minute.

Katie: Hello, Andrew. What's up?
Andrew: Not much. I'm phoning because I wanted to ask if we're going inline skating tomorrow afternoon.
Katie: Oh, that would be nice.
Andrew: What time can we meet?
Katie: Say four o'clock, in the park.
Andrew: Great. See you tomorrow. Bye.
Katie: Thanks for calling. Bye.

Wichtige unregelmäßige Verben

Infinitiv	Past Simple	Past Participle	Deutsch
be	was/were	been	sein
beat	beat	beaten	schlagen
begin	began	begun	beginnen, anfangen
bite	bit	bitten	beißen
blow	blew	blown	blasen
break	broke	broken	verbrechen
bring	brought	brought	herbringen
build	built	built	bauen
burst	burst	burst	platzen, reißen
buy	bought	bought	kaufen
catch	caught	caught	fangen
choose	chose	chosen	wählen
come	came	come	kommen
cost	cost	cost	kosten
cut	cut	cut	schneiden
do	did	done	tun, machen
draw	drew	drawn	zeichnen
drink	drank	drunk	trinken
drive	drove	driven	fahren
eat	ate	eaten	essen
fall	fell	fallen	fallen
feed	fed	fed	füttern
feel	felt	felt	fühlen
fight	fought	fought	kämpfen
find	found	found	finden
fly	flew	flown	fliegen
forget	forgot	forgotten	vergessen
freeze	froze	frozen	frieren, einfrieren
get	got	got	bekommen
give	gave	given	geben
go	went	gone	gehen
grow	grew	grown	wachsen
have	had	had	haben
hear	heard	heard	hören
hide	hid	hidden	verstecken

Infinitiv	Past Simple	Past Participle	Deutsch
hit	hit	hit	schlagen, treffen
hold	held	held	halten
hurt	hurt	hurt	verletzen
keep	kept	kept	behalten
know	knew	known	kennen, wissen
lay	laid	laid	legen
lead	led	led	führen, leiten
leave	left	left	verlassen
let	let	let	lassen
lie	lay	lain	liegen
light	lit	lit	anzünden, beleuchten
lose	lost	lost	verlieren
make	made	made	machen
mean	meant	meant	bedeuten
meet	met	met	treffen
pay	paid	paid	bezahlen
put	put	put	setzen, stellen, legen
read	read	read	lesen
ride	rode	ridden	reiten
ring	rang	rung	klingeln
rise	rose	risen	aufgehen
run	ran	run	rennen
say	said	said	sagen
see	saw	seen	sehen
seek	sought	sought	suchen, erstreben
sell	sold	sold	verkaufen
send	sent	sent	schicken
set	set	set	setzen, stellen
shake	shook	shaken	schütteln
shine	shone	shone	scheinen
shoot	shot	shot	schießen, abfeuern
show	showed	shown	zeigen
shut	shut	shut	schließen
sing	sang	sung	singen
sit	sat	sat	sitzen
sleep	slept	slept	schlafen
speak	spoke	spoken	sprechen

Infinitiv	**Past Simple**	**Past Participle**	**Deutsch**
spend	spent	spent	ausgeben, verbringen
stand	stood	stood	stehen
steal	stole	stolen	stehlen
stick	stuck	stuck	befestigen, anheften
stink	stank	stunk	stinken
swear	swore	sworn	fluchen, schwören
sweep	swept	swept	fegen, kehren
swim	swam	swum	schwimmen
take	took	taken	nehmen, dauern
teach	taught	taught	unterrichten
tell	told	told	erzählen
think	thought	thought	denken
throw	threw	thrown	werfen
understand	understood	understood	verstehen
wear	wore	worn	tragen (Kleidung)
win	won	won	gewinnen
write	wrote	written	schreiben

Bildnachweis

DigitalStock: Seite 21 © M. Jakobi; Seite 65 © M. Zahrl; Seite 73 © J. Hilberger; Seite 77 © H. Walter

PantherMedia: Seite Seite 13 © Ludger Vorfeld; Seite 47 © Sigrid Link; Seite 53 © Jürgen von Wirth;

PIXELIO: Seite 20 © Thomas Max Müller

PHOTOCASE: Seite 41 © e-spresso; Seite 69 © designritter

Shutterstock: Seite 6 © Mark Yuill; Seite 10 © beaucroft; Seite 16 © Rafael Olkis; Seite 18 © 2265524729; Seite 25 © tony spuria; Seite 30 © Christoff; Seite 32 (links) © Rachael Grazias; Seite 32 (rechts) © Just ASC; Seite 35 © Andriy Rovenko; Seite 37 © Donald R. Swartz; Seite 38 © create-sima1; Seite 40 © Natalia Bratslavsky; Seite 43 © rfx; Seite 48 © javarman; Seite 55 © TechWizard; Seite 57 © Bryant Jayme; Seite 60 © Byron W. Moore; Seite 63 © James Steidl; Seite 75 © Cousin_ Avi; S. 95 Jozsef Szasz-Fabian

www.fotolia.de: Seite 5 © TimeHacker; Seite 12 © Jose Gil; Seite 36 © Rob Byron; Seite 42 © jeff gynane; Seite 67 © Mike Norton; Seite 83 © gajatz: Seite 84 © rimglow; Seite 89 © Mark FGD; Seite 91 © sonya etchison; Seite 94 © starekase; Seite 102 © David Turner; Seite 113 © Albo; Seite 119 © AndreasEdelmann; Seite 126 © auris

Stichwortfinder

Was haben dieser Elefant und diese Schüler gemeinsam?*
*Das Gelernte ist im Langzeitgedächtnis
Deutsch:
5. Klasse
Mathe:
6. Klasse
Englisch: sehr gut
7. Klasse
Mit Download für phase-6
mentor
- Coole Lernhilfe mit Download
- Mit phase-6 einfach ins Langzeitgedächtnis
Ein Fach, eine Klasse, ein Band - inklusive elektronische Karteikärtchen für phase-6 zum Downloaden. So kannst du den Schulstoff wirklich verstehen und garantiert behalten. Ab August 2009 auch für die 8. Klasse.
Weitere Infos unter www.mentor.de/sehr-gut
mentor
Eine Klasse besser.